ATTRACTING
ROMANCE

by

Lowell Jay Arthur

dp
DISTINCTIVE PUBLISHING CORP.

Attracting Romance
By Lowell Jay Arthur
Copyright 1992 by Lowell Jay Arthur

Published by Distinctive Publishing Corp.
PO Box 17868
Plantation, Florida 33318-7868
Printed in the United States of America

ISBN: 0-942963-20-2
Library of Congress No.: 92-6891
Price: $14.95

Library of Congress Cataloging-in-Publication Data

Arthur, Lowell Jay, 1951-
      Attracting romance / by Lowell Jay Arthur.
          p.   cm.
      Includes bibliographical references.
      ISBN 0-942963-20-2 : $14.95
      1. Interpersonal relations. 2. Interpersonal communication. 3. Love.
      4. Self-actualization (Psychology)   I. title.
      HM132.A76   1992
      306.7—dc20   92-6891
                                                                CIP

Attracting Romance

Table of Contents

Preface   1
1. Winning Through Attraction   7
   The World is Flat 10
   Change is Constant 11
   Success is an Adventure 13
   Ordinary Magic 19
2. Fear and Loathing on the Romance Trail 23
   Health and Stress 28
   The Hero 31
   Me and My Shadow 32
   Obstacles to Self-esteem and Success 34
   Worry 38
   Hate 39
   Guilt 41
   Misery Loves Company 42
   Inventing Your Future 44
3. Wizards and Magicians 47
   Self-Deprivation 50
   Loneliness 51
   Victims, Dragons, and Saviors 52
   Warriors and Magicians 52
4. Claim Your Power 57
   Follow the Yellow Brick Road 57
   Define Your Purpose 59

Give Yourself Permission 60
Choose Your Goals 61
Build a Plan 65
Take Action 68
Develop Persistence 71
Achievement 72
5. What You See is What You Get 75
Visual, Auditory, and Kinesthetic 77
Creative Visualization 79
Dreaming 87
6. I Think, Therefore I Am 91
Beliefs 94
Let's Talk 96
The Irresistible Law of Attraction 97
Good Thought, Bad Thought 98
Mind Poverty 99
Mental Wealth 100
7. Cast it in Concrete 103
Self Management 104
Self Programming 105
Affirmation 106
Imprinting 108
Cement Factories of the Mind 110
8. The Hero's Journey 113
Innocent 114
Orphan 114
Martyrs 115
Wanderers 115
Warrior 116
Magicians 117
The Part-That-Knows and the Part-That-Drags 117
Metamorphosis 118
Have Faith 119
Alignment 120
Intuition 122
Foundation 124
9. The Communication Challenge 127
Personality Types 128

What Communication? 131
Modeling and Acting 132
Mental Strategies 134
    Visual 136
    Auditory 136
    Physiology 137
Success Strategies 138
Love Strategies 139
Metaprograms 141
Clearing Negativity 144
10. Come to the Cabaret 149
Study and Learning 150
Failure 151
Intent 154
The Land of the Lounge Lizards 155
Salesmanship 157
How to Get Whatever You Want 158
It's Always Too Soon to Give Up 163
He Who Hesitates Waits 165
Rewards 168
11. In the Groove 171
The Past 174
In the Beginning 175
The Present 176
Getting Out 178
Side Dishes 179
12. Life Balance 183
Personal-Professional-Private 185
Body-Mind-Spirit 188
Male-Female 191
Meditation 192
Prayer 192
Balance 193
Appendix A - The Affirmations of Love 194
Appendix B - Quick Reference to the Success Exercises 197
Appendix C - Other Resources for Success 199

Preface

THIS BOOK IS ABOUT GETTING WHAT YOU WANT as a lover and a partner in a romantic relationship. Possibilities surround you now. It doesn't matter if your concept of getting what you want is marriage, companionship, love or sex; this book will help you get what you need. In these pages you'll learn how to go after the man or woman who looks, sounds, and feels like the person you really want. This book will not, however, teach you how to manipulate others into giving you what you want, because manipulation is unnecessary. Hundreds of people in your area crave exactly the kind of relationship that you do. Through the exercises in this book, you will learn how to pull these people into your life. This book will guide you through the inner work that will make romance blossom in your life now.

Abundance is your natural state. You can have many satisfying relationships—male-female, supervisor-worker, or friend-friend. It doesn't matter if you're rich or poor, beautiful or "ugly," sixteen or sixty. You can attract into your life the right man or woman to meet your current needs.

For example, men and women who have recently ended a relationship, whether it was a marriage or a long-standing romance, may not want to risk loving yet, but they still may need sex or intimacy or companionship. It doesn't matter. Hordes of single people want exactly the same thing you do. You don't have to be alone, but what you do need is a way to help attract these people into your life. This book will teach you the methods and tools to attract the right person

1

into your life. I'm not going to ask you to work hard, but I will ask you to work persistently. The tools are simple and easy to use. Have you ever noticed that if something is complex, it's usually part of the problem and if it's simple, it's usually part of the solution? This book is part of the solution to your romantic happiness. The rest is up to you.

For the moment, let's look at male-female relationships. Current literature suggests that if there's something wrong in a woman's life, it's a man's fault (and vice versa). If we could just bridge this chasm between men and women—a barrier to understanding—I believe that we could easily establish win-win relationships. Men and women obviously have different points of view. This is neither bad nor good; it just is. From the moment you are born, well meaning parents, family, and friends conspire to develop your masculinity or femininity. We all share male and female traits. The masculine, warrior side dominates in most males. The feminine, intuitive side has a caring, loving, nurturing nature. To be all that we can be, we need a balance of both masculine and feminine traits. When it comes to finding relationships, we are all looking for a man or a woman who can teach us about our atrophied masculine/feminine sides. We can learn to see our differences as an opportunity, not a liability, when it comes to understanding men and women and succeeding at romance.

Most women and a large percentage of men feel that it is difficult and uncomfortable to meet people: small talk, the crowded bar scene, the first dates, the blind dates, and on and on. A staggering amount of effort is wasted in these pursuits. Because of the discomfort, people often become exhausted with the process and settle for less than what they truly desire in a relationship.

Have you developed the habit of accepting whatever life dishes out? Have you accepted the average and ordinary instead of the great and the wonderful? Have you let life start running you? Do you feel as though, as P.T. Barnum would say, "There's a sucker born every minute. You just happened to be coming along at the right time"? Well, you don't have to endure relationships from hell, but if you do what you've always done, you'll get what you've always gotten. Your willingness to accept love will affect your abundance, health and prosperity. Refuse to tolerate anything that doesn't give you joy, happiness, and fulfillment.

Relationships should bring you freedom, a sense of flying, not floundering. Love is not scarce. It's easy to attract a perfect mate if you believe you can and you focus on what you *want*. If, however, you focus on all the times in the past when you "failed" in a relationship, you will tend to attract more failure. This book will give you the strategies for shifting from past failure to future success. Your days of hoping and worrying are over.

But, you might say, "I'm no good at this relationship stuff!" Well, it may appear that some people are more successful when it comes to relationships. When someone is good with people, everyone says, "He or she was born with it!" Nonsense. They just happened to develop these skills through trial and error or some ridiculous stroke of luck. You will discover, as I have, that these skills can be learned. Usually 50% of the success goes to 5% of the men and women, but success can have different meanings. One person may feel that having lots of sexual, romantic or marital partners is success. To others, it's having a solid marriage. To others, it's a date for the movies on Saturday night. There is no right or wrong, good or bad to these definitions. The only time there's a problem is when they conflict with your partner's definition of success. Sometimes our expectations of others blind us to their beauty.

You probably have a lot of skepticism about the claims made thus far. Good! Skepticism is a healthy approach to any new idea. Why, you might ask, was I given this clarity of understanding? If this is so simple, why hasn't it already been discovered by others? To some extent, it has. I have found references in many places, but no one has organized and presented the techniques. Here are a couple of thoughts that I've discovered by other skeptics:

> *Everything that can be invented, has been invented.*
> —Charles Duell, head of the U.S. Patent Office, 1899

> *I think there is a world market for about five computers.*
> —Thomas J. Watson, Jr., 1943

You might ask how I came into possession of the secrets of creating romantic success. Well, it wasn't easy. I was probably fourteen or fifteen the first time I wondered: "How can I meet someone who's not only attractive, but shares my interests, goals, and ambitions in life?" Getting someone who was attractive seemed tough enough; getting the whole package seemed impossible. That question nagged me for 20 years.

Over the years, I digested tomes of information on self-help, metaphysics, success, and relationships. I have to tell you that I had a healthy skepticism when I first started exploring these techniques for getting what I wanted out of life, but I did what I anticipate you will do. I suspended my disbelief and tried them out. Sometimes you have to look at the complexity to see the simplicity in things, and so it is with relationships. The more I learned, the less murky it became. It wasn't until several months after my marriage that the simplicity leaped out at me. Now I want to share what I've learned. Relationships are the key to success in life.

> **Success Secret:**
> We already have the tools
> to succeed at attracting romance.

I married my wonderful wife in the summer of 1988. I was a bachelor until the age of 36. Then about six months after we were married, I started thinking about how, after dozens of other relationships that didn't make it anywhere near the altar, I had so successfully acquired this union in my life. And there it was, a blinding flash of the obvious: we all have the tools to do this consistently. Everyone has all the resources they need to attract the opposite sex. You don't lack the resources to succeed; you lack access to and control of those resources. What you need is an owner's manual about how to get in touch with them and how to use them to achieve your goals.

You spent years in school pumping your analytical mind and learning how to get the *one right answer*, but you were expected to learn how to deal with people—parents, children, leaders, and lovers—through osmosis.

Success, fortunately, leaves clues. During 1990-1992, I spent more than 40 days developing mastery in an emerging science of communication excellence called NLP—Neuro-Linguistic Programming. This training helped me further understand how these tools and techniques for romantic success work. The earliest contributions of NLP were to describe the specific ways that people establish, maintain, and evolve relationships over time. NLP also offers ways to clearly and vibrantly describe our desires in ways that enhance our ability to attract romance. NLP also gives us important insights into the way to master our communications with others and to understand their internal values, beliefs, and experience so that we can create highly ecological, win-win relationships together. NLP makes the rather vague concepts of positive thinking and metaphysics into clearly understandable and applicable techniques for personal success and genius. After you have read this book and done the exercises, I believe that you will have seen, heard and felt the power of NLP to expand your abilities for all human endeavors, including attracting romance.

I believe that you already have all the resources you need to succeed in attracting romance. I don't guarantee to have all of the right answers, but I can help you gain access to the resources and control of the tools you already have, in ways that will make relationships blossom in your life now.

Chapter One

Winning Through Attraction

SOME OF YOU ARE LOOKING for a fulfilling relationship now. Some of you are already in relationships, but don't feel good about them. I don't know how many times I've been in both situations. I've had lonely periods and I've stayed in a relationship that wasn't going anywhere because I didn't know if I could find a better one. If you're in a similar situation, take heart. Using the skills in this book, you need never be alone, unless you choose to be. As you use this book and as you do the exercises, don't be surprised if your past dissolves and new relationships magically appear. As you clarify what you want from your life and release the old relationship garbage you're hoarding, people, places, and circumstances will change to make room for the improvements you desire. Everyone is inherently perfect, but some people are more perfect for you than others. Like clothes on a store mannequin, a person may look good, but not fit you very well. Or they might have an exciting voice, but not look right at all. The way you find the right man or woman for you is by changing your goals and desires.

> **SUCCESS SECRET:**
> You can change your internal autopilot!

I believe that people "work" perfectly; it's just that their internal programming is not ideal. Each of us has an internal autopilot that guides our life according to our values and beliefs. Like an iceberg, your conscious mind is clearly visible. The subconscious mind (about 80 percent) lies invisibly beneath your conscious awareness, directing most of your actions and behaviors. Everything you've experienced is a result of the values, beliefs and desires you've fed your subconscious mind over the years. For example, you may have turned away the love of a lifetime because the person contradicted your image of yourself at that time. As you learn to redirect your autopilot and give it new choices that are as good, if not better, than its old choices, you'll learn that you can solve any problem, overcome any obstacle to romantic success. Problem solving is creative! All you need are ways to solve your current lack of success. Changing your internal autopilot is the key to changing the results you're receiving in your life. Let's take a look at how you can begin to change your course.

SUCCESS SECRET:
Dress for an objective; success is already within you.

To be successful you're probably going to need to get rid of some preconceived notions about how people meet. Somewhere along the way, people and advertising convince us that to attract romance we need to dress a certain way, drive a certain kind of car, have a college education, or whatever. None of these things will hurt, but none of them is essential. I know divorced women with children who block their success by believing that no one would put up with their kids. (My wife has two from her first marriage.) Other people believe that they're too busy with a career: "No one would want the trivial amount of time I have to give." Nonsense. Some other person has exactly the same need.

I know people who prevent themselves from developing meaningful relationships by saying, "I have to be financially secure," but no matter how well they're doing, they never feel financially secure. Similarly, some women believe that the man should always initiate the contact. Because of this, women often believe that they have no control over who they meet. All of these beliefs block our success. If we believe that we're not good enough, we can find thousands of excuses for a lack of love in our lives. If, however, we decide that we deserve love in our lives, nothing can keep it out. Here's why!

There are two ways to get things in this world:

1. *Act!* Go out there and get it! This is the masculine, warrior perspective. Have you ever noticed, however, that whenever you use force to conquer your universe, it only creates resistance? Action is an important, but not the critical, key to success.

2. *Attract!* Pull into your life the people, places, events, and things that will fulfill you. Charm and charisma enchant males and females alike. Become a magnet for romance. Attraction is the feminine, magician perspective. The feminine always has more power than the masculine. Water is fluid and yielding (feminine), but it will wear away rock (masculine), which cannot yield.

SUCCESS SECRET:
You can **attract** perfect relationships into your life.

Of these two choices, *attraction is the strongest.* Attraction, as I mean it, doesn't involve physical attraction. Attraction is the magnetism that pulls positive relationships into your life. Attraction occurs when we put our needs out into the world so that the perfect person can be drawn into our lives. There are two views of how this occurs:

1. **The Force.** In *Star Wars*, Luke Skywalker uses "The Force" to defeat the Empire. The Force, as Obiwan describes it, is the connection among all living things. This is a key belief of all spiritual people. In other words, we are all connected by an invisible network. Some call this network God and others call it "Infinite Intelligence." By using this network, and by finding and building the right relationships in our lives, we support rightness in the whole world.

2. **Awareness** suggests that you can awaken yourself to the opportunities that swarm around you constantly. By releasing the hurt, anger, fear, frustration, beliefs, and values that blind you, and then by focusing on your desires, you will be able to first notice and then meet the attractive man or woman sitting in the corner of your favorite restaurant during lunch hour. Or you'll discover the romance of your dreams in the Impressionist section of your favorite museum. All you have to do is be open to what's already available.

Either of these two views is fine with me. I believe that they work together, in harmony, to bring us what we need. Of course, there are those people who doubt the existence of either. These are the same sort of people who cling to outmoded beliefs because they are widely accepted.

The World is Flat

In the days of Columbus, everyone believed that the world was flat — that if you sailed in any direction long enough, you would fall off. So, if attracting relationships is easy, why hasn't someone else figured out how to do it? Simple. Everyone still believes that it all happens by chance.

When it comes to relationships, we're still operating like the frog prince and Snow White. Men keep hoping that a princess will come along and kiss them, and the bewitched princess waits for a prince to awaken her from her dream. How much of your life have you wasted waiting for your prince or princess to appear?

I call this the Prince and Princess Charming trap. In this snare we wait for someone else to make our lives whole. This is nothing more than a love lottery. It's a product of "learned helplessness." As long as you wait for someone else to find you, you have no control. If you fail to set your own goals and directions, you will be swept along by the currents of others and washed up by the tide.

The first step is to heal yourself, to recognize that you are love energy. I say, kiss yourself! Awaken yourself! Be your own prince or princess. Design your own future.

"The best way to predict the future is to invent it!"
—Alan Kay

I agree. This is the only life you have to lead; you might as well live it your own way! One of the results of attracting romance is a quality of life that is buoyant, vigorous, simple, joyous, and passionate. Don't wait for your ship to come in; swim out to it! To really succeed at attracting romance, you will need to:

1. Take responsibility for your success in relationships.
2. Build your self-esteem.
3. Identify the obstacles you've built to your own happiness.
4. Change your thoughts, values, and beliefs.
5. Attract powerful relationships into your life.
6. Take action to achieve the happiness you so richly deserve.
7. Maintain and improve the relationships you develop.

There's at least one valid reason for doing these seven things: the mortality rate is three times higher for people with few close relationships. To pretend you are alone and not connected to society can cause grave problems. Finding the right relationships are as important to personal health and growth as nutrients are to the body. Community life helps immunize you against disease.

To achieve success in relationships, you will need stability, but you will also need to change.

Change is Constant

SUCCESS SECRET:
Develop a clear intent to succeed.

The only way to improve your life is to conceive a better one. I want to help you do just that. There is no problem or obstacle that cannot be overcome. One of the keys to success is a clear intention to succeed. I want you to become a master of *intent*. Intent consists of three elements—desire, belief, and acceptance.

1. **Desire** - a burning desire to have the love, sex, and companionship you deserve in your life. You must desire happy, fulfilling relationships. Mark Fischer said: "Desire is what best sustains your thoughts. The more passionate your desire is, the more quickly the thing you want will spring up in your life."

2. **Belief** - a solid belief that you *can* develop and *deserve* to develop satisfying relationships.

3. **Acceptance** - a willingness to accept perfect relationships in your life.

Most people have the desire, but as they progress through a series of relationships, they lose their belief in romantic success. Their self-esteem drops with each "failure" and when the right person comes along, they may not notice.

To begin to overcome your old baggage, I want you to do the following exercise right now and then *every morning and night* for seven days.

Exercise:
Read, say aloud, think, and write on paper the following:
I am willing to change.
I am willing to change the pattern of beliefs that have been blocking my romantic success.

This exercise is critical. If you haven't been in satisfying relationships, or if you have and they have fallen apart for some reason, it's a result of your current beliefs, thoughts, and feelings. If you use the same recipe, you'll eat the same meal. To succeed, you need to change those beliefs. Being willing to change is the first step.

I asked you to do this in four different ways:
Reading is a visual/analytical task that exercises one part of the brain and stores the message in your memory for later recall. By reading only, we absorb 10% of the message.
Speaking exercises another area of the brain and the vibrations of the sound echo through your entire body, helping to start the change. We retain 30% of what we read and hear.

Thinking these thoughts creates a powerful magnet in another part of the mind that will attract positive change into your life. We remember 70% of what we say to ourselves!

Writing is a mechanical task that exercises still another part of the brain (while exercising *reading* and *thought* at the same time). This is why written affirmations and statements are so important in changing your present circumstances. We retain 90% of what we do.

This will get the whole brain working on opening you up to change. Doing this exercise early in the morning when you rise and just before bed will further enhance its effectiveness. The analytical "left brain" and the creative "right brain" portions are more likely to be working together at these times. They will combine to achieve the changes you desire.

Readiness of the mind is wisdom. This exercise is the key to preparing the mind for what is to follow. The very fact that we desire change is a sure sign that we can change! I have found that success comes to the person who desires, believes in, and accepts opportunity.

Success is an Adventure

Attracting romance is an adventure, not a destination. Meeting someone is only one step of the challenge. Then you begin cultivating the relationship, contemplating marriage, and continuously evolving to meet each other's needs and desires.

Relationships are the most challenging and exciting activities you will ever undertake. Succeeding in a relationship, over time, will require your commitment and enthusiasm. There are many definitions of success.

Here are a few of my favorites:

SUCCESS means successful living—long periods of peace, joy, and happiness.

SUCCESS is the progressive realization of predetermined, worthwhile goals.

SUCCESS is divinely ordained. *"All things are yours."*

(I Corinthians 3:21).

Nothing succeeds like **SUCCESS**! - Ange Pitou

There's no deodorant like **SUCCESS**.

SUCCESS = what we know + what we do with what we know.

Unfortunately, an ordinary person usually takes everything as either a blessing or a curse. The soul of a free person looks at life as a series of problems, while the slave whines, "What can I do? I am but a slave." A warrior takes everything as a challenge . . . views everything as a mystery to be solved.

Which are you? A free person or a slave? A warrior or a whiner? Have you been blocking your own success by:

Hanging on to old beliefs and old relationships?
Expecting to receive love without first giving
something of value?
Seeking love outside yourself, instead of loving
the person within?
Seeking to change others instead of yourself?

Do not expect some other person to fulfill you. Seeking the light of love outside of yourself means there is a darkness within—a place where you do not love yourself. What you are seeking in any relationship is yourself. Your true nature is one of loving and learning. If you want to succeed at attracting romance, seek the barriers within yourself that prevent love from entering your life; then eliminate them.

Anything you want can come true if you cast it in terms of a concrete goal that you desire, believe in, and are willing to accept. You can always get what you want if: 1) you know what you want; 2) you know what you are willing to give in return; and 3) you are willing to help others get what they want.

SUCCESS SECRET:
Give others what they want.

We spend 95% of our time thinking about ourselves. To succeed at attracting the right man or woman into your life, you are going to have to start thinking about their needs, not yours. You will want to figure out what they want and how to give it to them, because that is the only way that you can get what you want.

Now, some of you may have a belief that all men want what feels good—sex, the height of physical experience—and that all women want things that look and sound good—gifts, flashy cars, and expensive entertainment. True, some men and women *do* want these things, but not *all*. Only a small minority want these extremes. Later in this book we'll discuss the three different communication styles—visual, auditory, and kinesthetic—in more detail. Visuals may like to take you places, buy you things, and so on. If this is what you want, you can use the tools in this book to help you attract the people and circumstances to meet these needs. But be careful what you ask for, because, as the old expression goes, "the gods may give it to you!" Auditories like the way things sound; they may enjoy concerts, live comedy, or anything that is music to their ears. Kinesthetic men and women will want to be touched in certain ways. They often enjoy sports. Most people are a combination of these styles and one will usually dominate their experience. Values and beliefs vary widely for these three styles. Regardless of style, however, all three enjoy the feeling of being loved.

SUCCESS SECRET:
Men and women want the feeling
they get when they're in love.

To build a relationship, you will need to help your partner experience this feeling! I have discovered, unfortunately, that most people are anxious to improve their lives as long as it doesn't require any effort. Like Dorothy in the *Wizard of Oz*, women may want a man with the Scarecrow's brain, the Tin Man's heart, and the Lion's courage. I doubt that such a new age superman exists, but I personally know women who are waiting to marry a man who earns a good living, a man with a future, a man with wealth. This is not a problem, but they are unwilling to develop the skills, the gifts, that such a man would require. Men want women who make them *feel* like men. The reverse is also true.

A man may want to marry a wealthy or beautiful woman, but may be unwilling to develop the skills to do so. Most women need communication, sensitivity, love, romance, sex, and compassion. What makes a gigolo so successful? Excellence at providing a woman with what she needs and wants. Let's face it; our society doesn't exactly train men to develop their feminine traits. Women want men who make them *feel* like women.

We all want to reaffirm our masculine or feminine side. Once we feel secure in our dominant roles, we can begin to explore our unfamiliar, undernourished, less dominant side.

Does this mean we must educate ourselves to meet the needs of other men or women? Yes, I believe it does. Novels are full of stories of men and women who rise from rags to riches, but these heroes and heroines don't get to the top by luck. Along the way, we see each of them gain the skills to achieve success. They work for what they get.

No one owes you a free ride! You have to give, and you should always try to give more than you expect to receive in return. This doesn't mean that you should stay in a bad relationship in which all you do is give and give. In a supportive relationship, however, I think you'll find that as you learn to give, your gifts will multiply and come back to you. To the extent that you are willing to develop your ability to help others get what they need, you will be able to get what you need.

I once dated a woman from Texas. One of her favorite things was country and western dancing. Well, I'd had ballroom dancing and various kinds of disco dancing, but never C&W. It took me some time to learn the two-step, waltz, and Cotton-eyed Joe. And then there was the ten-step and variations on all these themes. I have to admit that I've never felt totally natural with C&W, but I learned because it was important to her. That's one of the great things about relationships: they expose us to things we'd never otherwise attempt.

I had a friend who used to amaze me with the number and beauty of the women he dated. He dressed impeccably, drove Rolls Royces and Ferraris, lived in a beautiful home and loved to dance. Aside from his job, he constantly played the stock and real estate market to finance his dreams. He continuously fed his mind with the books, pictures, and thoughts that assured his success. He was willing to pay the price to achieve his personal, romantic, and financial goals. He had stumbled early on the secrets of success. He married an attractive woman and has several wonderful children.

Similarly, I know women who have a career, a family, *and* a successful marriage. They have gladly paid the price to succeed in each of these areas.

SUCCESS SECRET:
Decide to pay the price for creating successful relationships, and decide to pay in advance.

No matter what your definition of success may be, you will always have to pay the price to reach it and you'll always have to pay in advance. A field cannot yield a harvest unless you first sow the seeds of success. Then you will need to cultivate and encourage your growth. You cannot succeed until you learn the basics of attracting romance.

I recommend that you start a notebook for the exercises we'll do in the rest of the book. Open up a blank page of a spiral notebook now and do the following:

Exercise:
    a. What is your definition of success in romantic relationships? Take a few minutes and write down everything that comes to mind, no matter how preposterous or exotic.
    b. Next answer each of the following questions quickly:
        1. Do you really want to succeed with romance?
        2. What would make your relationship successful?
        3. Is it okay for you to find love, sex, and happiness?

4. Are there any internal objections to success? What are they?

5. Are you willing to pay the price of success?

6. Do you know how to love yourself?

7. Are you ready for romantic success?

8. Does your definition of success match your personality and life goals?

c. Think about your current love life. If there were a question that seemed to quietly guide all of your behavior, what would it be? (For example, mine was, "How can I meet someone who is not only attractive, but shares my interests, goals, and ambitions in life?") Imagine yourself in a romantic situation and notice if this question really fits. If not, change it until it does. Now modify the question to include all of the following and notice how that changes your experiences with the men and women you meet:

- The other person's needs

- *What* or *how* you can both succeed

- Present tense (as opposed to past or future)

d. Now think about your current love life. If there were a statement that seemed to quietly guide much of your behavior, what would it be? (For example, one woman always said, "All the best men are already married." She routinely got involved with married men.) How would you change this statement to your own benefit?

Back already? Good. In the second part of the exercise you may have discovered some beliefs or fears that are holding you back from romantic success, but if you truly desire a committed relationship, you'll attract someone who wants the same thing.

Your definition of success is what you need, and you deserve to have it in your life now ... if (and this is a BIG *if*) it's in your best interests *and* you're willing to accept it. Sometimes what we think we want in a relationship would not be good for us. In these situations, the man or woman we desire will not appear. Stop viewing these results as failure; they are feedback, no more, no less. Just change your desires. Don't feel bound to your definition of success; change it as your needs change. After all, it is *your* definition.

You must also be willing to accept success when it arrives! Some people I've worked with have had success strike quickly, and then, to my amazement, they can't believe it, and they go out of their way to sabotage their happiness. You have to be ready for success. The headlines are littered with men and women like Marilyn Monroe and John Belushi who weren't ready for success.

I think you'll find that when you desire something so completely that you are willing to stake your future on it, you are sure to win and help other special people win at the same time! Your definition of success in romantic relationships is the key to romance in your life. The remainder of this book will help you realize this goal through the application of what I call ordinary magic.

Ordinary Magic

> **SUCCESS SECRET:**
> You are a magnet!

The mind is the master weaver. You are constantly attracting people and events into your life. You already have everything you've programmed into your internal autopilot. If you aren't satisfied, then you will need to learn how to change your desires. Then you can attract whoever and whatever you need or want into your life. The trick is learning how to make your magnet work. Making it work is what I call ordinary magic. Everyone has these natural abilities.

For a plant or a stone to be natural is no problem. Being natural is something humans must work on. We need to be flexible. Unfortunately, given the choice between the safety and security of what we know and the growth we need, we often choose safety. John Grindner, a co-founder of Neuro-Linguistic Programming, has a good motto for these moments:

If you can, you can't.

If you can't, you must.

By this he means that if you can do something easily, then you need to stop relying on it for a while so that you can develop new choices. If you can't do something, however, you must do it because it will cause the greatest growth in your personal skills and abilities. For those of you who have an intense desire to overcome any barrier in your path, if you decide that there *is* a way to succeed and that it's the course you want to follow, victory and triumph are assured.

In the rest of this book we'll explore the keys to ordinary magic—intent, responsibility, self-esteem, visualization, thought, and affirmation. We'll look at ways to attract people into our lives and ways to go out and find them.

You'll know you've mastered attracting romance when it's no longer a concern in your life.

Chapter Two

Fear and Loathing on the Romance Trail

You gain strength, courage, and confidence by every experience in which you really stop to look fear in the face. You must do the thing you think you cannot do.
—Eleanor Roosevelt

L IFE WILL GIVE YOU WHATEVER YOU'RE WILLING TO accept. To be willing to receive these things into your life, you will need self-esteem. Nobody has self-esteem and self-confidence when they enter this life. High self-esteem only comes from confronting and handling life's challenges, not from taking an easy, do-nothing attitude. If you cultivate self-respect and inner security, you can meet anyone, have as much money as you need, and succeed in any way. Success begins from the inside and works its way out!

Self-esteem is our earliest verdict, our earliest judgement about ourselves. In school, we learn that we're an *A, B,* or a *C* student. Unfortunately, many of us took these as measures of our self-worth, not our abilities or our interests in a particular subject. From our parents and friends we got various judgements: "She's a klutz." "He's going to be a quarterback." "She'll be a great mother." We take all of this in, especially since it comes from the authority figures in our lives, and start repeating it to ourselves. "Whoops, dropped a pencil;

23

Mom was right, I am a klutz." Pretty soon, what do you know, we go out of our way to be a klutz.

Friends and family don't mean to program you in this way. As soon as they see someone do something more than once, they start to make judgements. In my case, my key skill was to stand up suddenly and hit my head on a cabinet door or the underside of a table. This happened on various occasions over the years and my mom started to say, "He's always hitting his head." She was right. I started hitting my head on all kinds of things. To this day, I'll do it occasionally, and I'll still hear her voice say, "He's always hitting his head."

I call these beliefs, *belief baggage*. They're things about ourselves that aren't true, but we've come to believe that they are.

Exercise:

> Dig up some key belief you have about yourself, listen to what you say to yourself about this belief, and listen to who's talking. Is this a belief you want to hang on to or not?

A belief that most people share is that men should be self-assured, unafraid, and in control. Surprisingly enough, most men are easily hurt. If you don't believe me, look at the effort we expend not to show it. From the **Hite Report on Male Sexuality**, I discovered that 61% of men often felt hurt, but didn't show it. Most men are sensitive. 62% said they would like for women to make passes at them! 87% were concerned with success in business. 99% rated sex as important, but overrated (65%). Most had some anxiety about their sexual performance. Examining these few figures, it's possible to see why most men develop insecurities around the male stereotype. Insecurity is one of the hallmarks of low self-esteem.

People with low self-esteem come in two varieties: aggressive and timid. The typical macho man, for example, probably has a low sense of self-worth. He's likely to be arrogant, domineering, and boastful—a rebel. Aggressive men and women with low self-esteem tend to be impatient, compulsive, perfectionists; nothing is ever good enough, including their own efforts. These people can rarely admit their mistakes.

Timid people are anxious and limp of hand, with weak voice, and wavering eye contact. We've all had times when our self-esteem is low and we exhibited some of this behavior. We can, however, decide to change, and the fastest way to do this is to change our physiology: stand or sit up straight, breathe deeply, smile, and look up. Do this for ten seconds now. That makes you feel better, doesn't it? That's why Dale Carnegie says, "Act enthusiastic and you'll be enthusiastic!" Change your body and you'll change your internal experience.

What other things separate successful people with high self-esteem from the failures with a low self-concept? A few simple things:

1. Failures ignore their successes. Instead, they reminisce, replay, and repeat their failures over and over again on the screen of their mind. Failures also "blow the problem out of proportion," making it bigger, brighter, more vivid, and closer instead of farther away, smaller, darker, and dimmer. As we'll see in successive chapters, this imprints the mind with failure tapes that play over and over again. Successful people keep their successes big, bright, and right in front of them. Successful people replay these movies over and over again in their mind. They put their failures *behind* them and ask: "What can I learn from this?" Successful people view each failure from a distance so that they can see it as a learning experience and nothing more.

2. Failures try to achieve huge, flashy successes. If they succeed, they view it as luck. They rarely ask themselves: "What did I do to make this happen?" When they fail, as they usually do, they thrash in the swamp of their failure, blame others, and, instead of learning anything, jump on the next train to apocalyptic success. Insecure people grasp at grand and glorious leaps of self development. The desire to impress people fails to improve their quality of character or life. Those who achieve sudden success, but aren't prepared, often go to extremes to balance the scales. For example, consider John Belushi, Marilyn Monroe, Janis Joplin, and so on. When it comes to financial riches, many people make and lose several fortunes before they become comfortable with success. Walt Disney went bankrupt once on his route to success.

One woman I dated in the early 1980's fell into the failure category. She went to Washington, D.C., to be at the seat of the nation's power. After struggling there for a while, she returned to Colorado. She tried for one big score after another, sometimes in oil and at other times in various get-rich-quick schemes. After we'd gone separate ways for more than a year, she called me on the day she'd lost a particularly good job, invited me over for dinner, and attempted to seduce me. Fortunately, I had the good sense to resist and, instead, I helped her work through what went wrong.

There is no failure, only feedback.

Failure is something which you need to eradicate from your vocabulary and your life.

Exercise:
On a scale of one to ten, rate your approach to success:

    1   2   3   4   5   6   7   8   9   10
The "Big Win"   Steady Progress

Based on this analysis, what do you need to do to become successful at attracting romance? Do you try to move too quickly toward the bedroom or the altar? Or, do you let relationships unfold like the petals of a flower?

When you get into romantic situations, do you feel confident and self-assured or nervous and insecure? If your tiny internal voice says, "It'll be all right; don't worry," and there's a tenseness in your stomach, you'll probably feel insecure. If you're like me, some days you are extremely confident, but, on others, fatigue makes cowards of us all. When you're insecure, you cannot attract what you *want*, only what you already *believe* you can receive. You've got to start believing you're special. The key to self-confidence is to start doing something special with your life, whether it's starting a good career or building a special relationship.

SUCCESS SECRET:
Replay your successes, not your failures.

Exercise:

Remember a time when you were successful at talking to, meeting, or dating someone. As you remember that time now, bring the images closer, make them brighter and more vivid, add sounds and music that match the mood. Now, if you haven't already, turn the images into a movie and step into it so that you see, hear, feel, smell, and taste the experience.

Now remember a time when you were not successful. Make this image a small, black-and white snapshot, see yourself in the picture, push it farther and farther away until you can look at it without discomfort. Now ask yourself, "What can I learn from this experience?" Once you've discovered what you can learn from this feedback, you can decide what to do with the picture. Either leave it where it is; have it go farther out until it is a tiny speck that burns up in the sun; or, if it is a particularly "bad" memory, imagine the picture on a pane of glass and shatter this image with a hammer.

Successful people move continuously toward their goals and celebrate the little successes they have along the way. Success is easy, not tough. We think it's hard because we need an excuse to explain our "failures." If a successful person runs into a roadblock, they look for a way around, through, under or over the obstacle. Successful people learn from every failure and every success.

Exercise:

Start saying the following as often as possible, especially before you enter a situation where you'll be toe-to-toe with a man or woman who you want to meet:

I'm the best; I'm the best; I'm the best. I'm the most loving, romantic man/woman that anyone could ever want. I'm the best!

Hint: If you do this often enough, you'll begin to believe it and attract others that believe it too.

SUCCESS SECRET:
There's nothing **wrong** with you now.

Exercise

Stand in front of a mirror, look directly into your eyes, and say, as honestly as possible, "I love you! I love and accept you exactly as you are!" Do this mentally anytime you are confronted with a mirror and your self-image will improve rapidly. As your self-image improves, you will improve as well.

You may consider this exercise narcissistic, but high self-esteem is not egotistical. Paradoxically, people with high self-esteem always tend to help other people; they never criticize. A person who acts superior never is. Men or women who act superior separate themselves from others. Isolation usually causes rigidity and death.

We are all faced with a series of great opportunities—brilliantly disguised as insoluble problems.
                                        —John Gardner

You can gain self-esteem by becoming aware of your strengths and by dealing with the very things you find most difficult. You can learn by observing and doing. For the moment, recognize that you can always improve and there's nothing wrong with you now. You are the best person you know how to be at this moment in time. Accept your greatness. Realize that before you can change the world and take care of others, you must first learn to take care of yourself.

Health and Stress

You can succeed in love, sex, and romance more easily if you feel healthy and energized. This means that you have to learn how to manage stress. You may need to: exercise; make time to be quiet or meditate; change your diet; or change your perception of life (See Figure 2.1).

I have found that walking or jogging on a regular basis keeps my stress down. B vitamins seem to be a requirement of mine as well. Ask yourself, "What do I need to do to have more energy and become more attractive?" As you exercise, relax, or eat better foods, you will begin to feel energized. If you're not eating the right foods, you'll feel your energy drop soon after you consume them. Learn to manage your body's energy by monitoring how you feel after you eat, drink, and exercise. Then change your behavior to cut out self-defeating activities.

The mind and body act on each other in remarkable ways. Scientists have determined that there is a feedback loop from the body to the mind and back again. Your emotional states affect your

Our Main Problem is

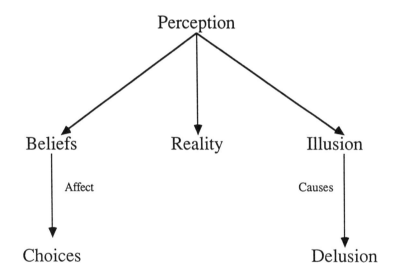

Stress is caused by our perception of an event.

Figure 2.1

immune system. Higher rates of illness occur among people who lose a relationship, mate, or spouse. Positive mental states, on the other hand, encourage health and longevity.

As I've mentioned before, people without friends, family and relationships are three times as likely to die early. People who are habitually pessimistic and have learned to feel helpless about changing their lives are more likely to neglect their health and do less to prevent unpleasant future events. There are documented cases of Aids patients living ten years or more. Aids carriers with a hardy psyche and even a touch of narcissism seem to bolster their immune system and stave off the disease. If attitude can help manage a disease like Aids, why can't it help you with the common cold?

The science of mental healing goes back more than 5,000 years. Many authorities expect mind-body healing to be the next revolution in Western medicine. As they say about ulcers: it's not what you eat; it's what's eating you.

Much of what we experience as loneliness, grieving or helplessness is stress. One simple system for stress management suggests that we should never sweat the small stuff. Then all we have to do is realize that *it's all small stuff*. For example, I was in an accident in 1975 that wrecked my new car and sent me to the hospital with a skull fracture. (No, that's not where I get all these weird ideas.) At the time, it seemed like the greatest trauma of my life; now, it seems like ancient history, something that could have happened to the Greeks or Romans.

If you find yourself depressed, try the following:

1. Do something! You can't be depressed when you're in motion and active.

2. Sit up or stand up straight, breathe deeply, and look up. You can't feel depressed in this physiology.

3. Lay out activities, both fun and work related, for the next several weeks so that you have something to look forward to doing.

This means that stress management is up to you. You have to take responsibility for letting yourself be depressed or hurt or angry. You have to take charge of your life. You have to become your own hero or heroine.

The Hero

> **SUCCESS SECRET:**
> Be yourself!

Some people, especially women — often want to be rescued because they do not know that they can rescue themselves. The hero or heroine, in all mythology, books, and movies, overcomes obstacle after obstacle and through these trials grows as a person. In this way, each of us is the hero or heroine of our own movie or romance novel. By facing our trials, we can grow and become the best person we can be.

Conform and be dull.
—J. Frank Dobie

Bravery is a willingness to be yourself, not what someone else wants you to be. By being yourself, you often open yourself to criticism and controversy from friends and family, but the only way to avoid controversy is to be mediocre, average, ordinary, and innocuous. You may often care too much about what others will think or say, thereby robbing your personal power. What's right for you isn't necessarily going to be popular with anyone else.

If you measure success in terms of praise and criticism, your anxiety will be endless.

—John Heider

Other people may criticize you. Often, however, these people are a reflection of a criticism you have of yourself. Evaluate if there is something you don't love about yourself and either start loving it or change it to match your needs. For example, I was at a bar one evening. I walked by three guys and the tallest had a thick mane of chocolate brown hair—hair I would love to have. He said to me, "Hey, I've read your book!"

"Really, that's great," I replied.

"Yeah, *Bald at Thirty*," he said.

I answered, "Oh, I thought you meant one of my published books." All of a sudden, he realized that I *am* an author and that he was joking around at my expense. He apologized and I made a note to start loving all the hair I have, because hating it can only make it fall out faster.

Exercise

Ask yourself, "What don't I like to be teased about?" Whatever comes up will be an area of low self-esteem. Recognize these areas, learn to love them the way they are, and start to improve these areas now.

If you are open to the available opportunities, you can learn from other's criticism and you may also teach the people who criticize you. Whenever anyone tries to attack your self-esteem, ask yourself, "Is there something I don't like about myself?" and, at the same time, help the other person learn something about their behavior. If you are attacked, act in a way that will shed light on the event. See every encounter as a dance, not a threat to your ego. The greatest martial arts allow your attacker to fall down. Your attacker is invariably off-center and vulnerable. Ease them to the mat!

Me and My Shadow

Your true relationship is with yourself. As you learn to love yourself, others will automatically learn to love you.

If you . . .	then others will . . .
hurt yourself	hurt you
criticize yourself	criticize you
respect yourself	respect you
trust yourself	trust you

Any time you put someone else down, you lower yourself as well. When you blame someone else, you give away your power. Self-acceptance means accepting others without judgement; often you secretly fear what you attack. For example, making fun of people who weigh more than you do is just a reflection of your fear of becoming heavy. Your safety lies in truth. You can only see beauty as beauty because there is ugliness. When you see the perfection in a person, you also find it in yourself. Anything you admire in another person, you have the ability to develop. The world consists of polarities. Like the north pole and the south pole, there are the rich and the poor, the beautiful and the ugly, the fat and the thin. Do not condemn someone for being rich or beautiful or thin. Rejoice in the success of others. As you focus on the people around you who succeed at finding and building great relationships, you'll begin to attract abundance into your life. If you focus on wealth or beauty or love, you'll attract them to you.

To give you an example, people often approach me tentatively and say: "I've been thinking about writing a book." They remind me of 1980 when I first started writing. Do you know what I tell them? "THAT'S GREAT! What's it about? What have you written so far?" I continue to nudge would-be authors toward their first book. Just because I've succeeded in publishing a book doesn't mean that someone else has to lose for me to win. There's lots of room for everyone. Similarly, just because I got married doesn't mean that there are fewer "good" women and that the chances for my single friends are diminished. Rejoice in the success of others and you'll attract it to yourself, quickly.

SUCCESS SECRET:
Surround yourself with winners.

Speaking of friends, an environment that creates winners is almost always made up of winners. Avoid "negative" people at all costs, even if it means dropping friends, relatives, and current lovers. You know the kind of people I'm talking about: people who have 101 reasons why you can't do something. You cannot be your best when the air around you is polluted with negativity. Guard yourself!

As you eliminate negativity in your life, you'll start to have the time to treat yourself well.

Exercise:
For a day, treat yourself the way you would want your lover to treat you. Would they take you to a beautiful resort in the mountains or by the shore? Would they feed you succulent lobster while planning a midnight bath with champagne? Do this for yourself. Plan it now and do it soon.

This exercise gets the male and female aspects of your *self* working together. Once you build an inner balance that supports you, you'll easily attract people to build your life. To love yourself is to heal yourself!

Exercise

In your notebook, list every significant thing you did or learned during each decade of your life. I, for example, found out that I've learned how to walk, ride a bicycle, read and write, kiss, cook, play guitar and banjo, drive, make love, and so on.

Now list everything you want to do in the next ten years. Hallucinate floridly!

> *If you can, you can't. If you can't, you must!*
> —John Grindner

Your uniqueness is your greatest asset, your value to the world. You will gain self-esteem by becoming aware of your strengths and by dealing with the very things you find most difficult. To continuously stretch your abilities, use John Grindner's suggestion: if you can easily do something one way, take away that choice for a day and find three new ways to do it. For example, if you are good at initiating conversation in a crowded elevator, then spend a day starting conversations on open street corners, in restaurants, or on public transportation. To further stretch yourself, if you can't do something, make it something that you must do within the next week. Force yourself to try things that presently make you uncomfortable. Your unique differences are the rare things that others need most.

Obstacles to
Self-Esteem and Success

Failure lowers our self-esteem; feedback and success build it. Sometimes, just by identifying what we're doing that has failure written all over it, we can begin to release the behaviors that are holding us back. To help you in this area, I'd like to provide the following steps to failure:

1. Fail to decide what you want from life.
2. Fail to set goals to get what you want.
3. Fail to plan a path to achieve these goals.
4. Procrastinate rather than activate.
5. Be indecisive rather than decisive.
6. Make excuses instead of making tracks.
7. Be indifferent to your own success rather than rewarding it.
8. Blame others instead of evaluating yourself for your lack of success.
9. Be wishy-washy instead of committed about your desires.
10. Spend your time wishing instead of fishing for success.
11. Compromise your goals and desires.
12. Quit before you succeed.
13. Search for shortcuts and quick fixes.
14. Refuse to act because someone might criticize you.

SUCCESS SECRET:
Failure is the foundation of success.

The creative process starts with energy—thought, visualization, intent, attitudes, and emotions—which create the experiences we desire based on the choices we make. The stairway to success is like flypaper—most people get stuck at one point or another because the major obstacle to success is yourself—your thoughts, beliefs and emotions. Our lack of education about interpersonal communication and attracting romance has woven a web of doubt. Life, however, doesn't have to be a struggle. By mastering our emotions, we can master our destiny.

In Napoleon Hill's classic book, *Think and Grow Rich*, he describes the seven positive and negative emotions:

Positive	"Negative"
Desire	Fear
Faith/Belief	Jealousy
Love	Hatred
Sex	Revenge
Romance	Greed
Enthusiasm	Superstition
Hope	Anger

If we desire, believe and anticipate that love, sex, and romance will enter our life, they will. If we are fearful, angry, mad, jealous or vengeful, they cannot.

The other side of every fear is freedom.
—Alan Watts

The big daddy of these "negative" emotions is fear. Actually, these emotions are neither positive or negative. Our response to them determines their impact. Fear, for example, can breed indecision, doubt, worry, indifference, caution, and procrastination. Fear can drain your batteries, create imaginary difficulties, and spread like disease. Fear can also be a powerful motivator to drive us toward success. We are born with the fear of falling and the fear of loud noises; every other fear we learn from others. We learn to fear death, criticism, old age, ill health, and loss of a loved one. Few people learn how to use the darker emotions as a spring board to success. Unfortunately, fear usually causes tension and inaction. Without action, we cannot turn our dreams into reality.

SUCCESS SECRET:
Fear is always an invitation to growth.

Men fear intimacy. The thought of committing to someone raises major fears, even in women. Women often fear being alone (an old maid), and deep within our psyche we often fear that we don't deserve love and prosperity. We can become convinced that we will pay dearly for our pleasures and, because we believe we will pay, we usually set up the people, places, events, and things to ensure that the price of pleasure is high instead of free.

Poor or unpleasant relationships drain our self-esteem. One reason people stay in bad or disappointing relationships is fear. We're afraid to hurt the other person or we're afraid they'll hurt us, or we're afraid we will end up alone, without a clue to finding another relationship. Using the tools in this book, you will never be alone and you will always attract important, dynamic, satisfying relationships. When it comes to getting out of poor relationships, remember that by getting out, you can help yourself and that other person get exactly what you both really desire—the feeling of a vital, exciting relationship!

The reason it takes people so long to get out of a stagnant marriage or relationship is that it's easier to stay with something you know than to risk the unknown. Your fears can outweigh your desires. Often, you're barely getting enough of what you need to keep you in the relationship. I call these relationships the *49 percent solutions*. You're getting almost enough to make it worthwhile, but not enough to feel the way you want to feel.

Why not attract a new relationship that gives you 80-90 percent? You may have to release the old one before there is room for the new, but why not have what you truly desire? If making the big leap seems too frightening, then decide to ease into it. If you're as uncomfortable as I am with leaping into the future, wade into it. Start practicing the exercises in this book and your old relationship will dissolve of its own accord, or it will start to evolve into what you want.

Another fear is the fear of failure. What if I talk to this person and they snub me, ridicule me, flog me? What then? Just remember that there are two kinds of failure:

1. Errors that you make when you try something new.
   Let's call these *feedback*.
   You can learn from feedback.

2. The failure of doing nothing at all.

I cannot tell you the number of times that I have seen a woman whom I found attractive, someone that my intuition said, "Yes, this woman would be a good choice!" and then I let fear get in the way.

I started playing the "what if" game. What if she says no? What if she gives me one of those hard "get lost" looks? I'd work myself into a frenzy about what could go wrong instead of what could go right. Later I would flog myself mercilessly for missing an opportunity.

On the other hand, when I gave fear no place to grow, I met some of the most interesting women. After mastering your fear and succeeding, you'll feel elated!

Exercise:

The next time you're tempted to avoid something (including a man or woman whom you want to meet) because of fear:

1. Say to yourself: "I will master this fear."
2. Start imagining everything going right.
3. Do what you fear.
4. Then reward yourself for doing it, whether you succeed or not.

For example, I feared drawing ridicule for writing this book, but I also felt that it was the essence of a self-help manual that I could have used to enrich my life much sooner. So I wrote it anyway and rewarded myself accordingly.

Exercise:

In your life now, what would you attempt if you knew you could not fail? Write the answer in your workbook. Who would you attempt to meet, if you knew you could not fail? Write this answer down and try to meet them today or tomorrow. Don't be shocked if you succeed, and then reward yourself for making the attempt, regardless of the result.

Worry

Another major form of fear is worry. We worry about our future, about death, and old age. Worry comes from indecision.

Humans are, by nature, lazy and indifferent. If you don't craft your future, someone else will do it for you. Then you will need to worry, because you're relying on chance to bring about a miracle. You have to invent your own future.

For example, if you believe in reincarnation, the lazy, indifferent human in you may say: "Well, I'll get it right in the next incarnation." On the other hand, we can recognize that we are here to learn. We can decide to learn as much as we can in this lifetime or we can spend more lifetimes going through all this turmoil again.

Or, if you prefer to see death as the end of life, then you deserve to get the most out of this life, right here and right now. You deserve the best that life has to offer. Demand it now!

There is no reason to fear old age. The only alternative is death and we've already decided that death isn't a viable option. I have a pet theory that the reason men age gracefully and women don't is that women worry about growing old. Men don't. What you fear or worry about you attract into your life; so stop worrying and start living. Revel in the dance of existence!

As I've said before, it doesn't matter if you're eight or eighty. If you want a satisfying relationship in your life, it's out there waiting for you. All you have to do is learn how to attract it into your life. No matter how old you are, you don't have to be alone.

A friend's grandmother lived into her nineties. If you were sixty and knew you were going to live another thirty years, wouldn't you want to try another career, have one more romance, celebrate the dance of life? I know I would. You never can tell if you're sixty years old or sixty years young.

I've known women who go into convulsions over their thirtieth birthday. They haven't found a man or they haven't started a family. I say set goals, develop and execute a plan. You're thirty years young!

Hate

Another potential obstacle to your success is hate or resentment toward a past lover or a spouse or yourself. When you are full of hate or anger toward someone, you have no room for love. Hating yourself will make you ugly.

People who hate or resent their parents may attract people into their lives who give them a weapon to further punish their parents, but rarely do they receive the love they need. Do you want to hurt others or find the love you deserve? If you're a self-proclaimed rebel, examine your goals and the actions you've taken. You may be asking for the love you need, but looking where it cannot be found.

The day I left Tucson for Denver, my dad took me aside and said, "Son, in six months you're going to be married, because you're just like your old man . . . you need someone to cook and clean and take care of you." Well, I showed him! I wasn't like him. I was my own man and I was damned well going to prove it. It took me fifteen years to stop rebelling and start deciding what I wanted for myself.

A little piece of advice: Don't wait that long. Start deciding today.

SUCCESS SECRET:
Forgive everyone who may have
"harmed" you in the past.

No one can hurt you but yourself. If one lover leaves, it's because a better one will appear. You need to forgive everyone from the past or present for any hurts, real or imagined, that you've received. To this idea, some of you will say: "Forgive the S.O.B! I'd like to kill him (or her)!" You are never upset for the reason you think you are; you're usually mad at yourself for not loving yourself and getting into a relationship that reinforced that belief. I know it's hard to understand, but forgiveness offers you a chance to:

1. **Release this person** from your life and make room for someone better.

2. **Improve your health**, because much ill health is caused by anger and resentment and hate held in the body.

3. **Learn from those relationships** because past relationships are a rich source of feedback from which to learn and grow.

I've used the following exercise successfully in my life. I got it from Louise Hay's excellent book and cassette series, *You Can Heal Your Own Life*. It has helped me be more healthy and attract better relationships in my life.

Exercise:

> Make a list of everyone, past or present, who has hurt you in any way. Then, on a frequent basis, say the following: The person I need to forgive is _____ and I need to forgive them for _____. What I learned from this experience is _____. I fully and freely release _____. May they go on to greater good.

You'll know you've cleared the negativity when you no longer feel anger boiling up when you think about this person. The first few times you do this, it will seem incredibly foreign, but with time, you'll learn to see each person as what they are, a teacher. The lessons were sometimes tough to learn, but they were important to your development.

Guilt

Another major roadblock is guilt. You can feel guilty about being loved, because you were never loved. You can feel guilty about loving sex, because your mother told you not to. You can feel guilty about not enjoying sex, when your partner wants you to. You can feel guilty that you had to end a relationship and "hurt" someone.

The *Course in Miracles* suggests that guilt is totally insane. I agree. Guilt blocks your ability to successfully attract romance. To feel guilty you have to beat yourself up in the present about something that happened in the past.

Guilt is usually a result of *dos, don'ts,* and *shoulds*: "*Be* careful! *Don't* have sex! *Don't* do that!" "You *should* do this or you *should* do that." *Shoulds* are other people's rules that you've imposed on your life. For example, I could say, "You should do every exercise in this book!" Nonsense. You could if you wanted to, but you might choose to do the ones that seem the most beneficial to you. Or you might choose to do none of them.

The same is true with relationships. How many times have we heard, "You should've stayed with Harry or Mary or whoever." Ridiculous! You deserve the best in life. You could've stayed with that person, but you chose to find a more rewarding relationship. This brings us to another important obstacle.

Misery Loves Company

SUCCESS SECRET:
Choose your friends wisely.

"No one wants a divorced woman/man with children." "He's bad for you." "All the best men/women are married." "All men are bastards."

I hear groups of men and women lamenting how awful it is out there in the cold, cruel world. The reason they can't find someone is because there's no one to be found. They criticize the men and women they see: too short, too fat, too ugly, too poor, too rich, too ... too ... too. People seek to discredit before they learn to trust.

You cannot attract what you criticize, condemn, complain about, or envy. What you give out, multiplies and comes back to you. When you criticize another person, you only hurt yourself. So give out only love.

Exercise:
Spend one entire day without criticizing, condemning or complaining about anyone or anything. (It's not easy.)

Some major obstacles to success are caused by
1. lack of trust;
2. not knowing what you want;
3. fear of the consequences of your actions (commitment, pregnancy, etc.);
4. fear of the new;
5. fear of other people's opinions.

This brings us to another fear—the fear of criticism. How do the friends in your "support" group talk? Do they talk of *lack*—how few men or women there are—or do they talk about *abundance*—how many available women or men there are? Are you afraid to approach a man or a woman, or even to develop a relationship for fear you will be criticized, rejected, or ostracized by your peers? We are all subject to the negative and positive attitudes of our friends and family.

During my freshman year in college I dated a wonderful woman. She was Catholic and I was raised Methodist. This didn't bother us, but it sure bothered our parents. It became clear that neither my mom nor her's approved. Looking back I can see that they were more afraid of losing us than of our differing backgrounds. We succumbed to parental pressure and broke up.

In later years, I found myself in the power of several people who groused about the availability of women in the local area. I found that it's a lot easier to say there are no available men or women than it is to take action and risk meeting someone new. Is *your* support group holding you back?

Exercise:

Go somewhere and do something you love to do at least once a month, but leave your friends at home. See if you don't feel more free to actively meet other people, men and women. If your company loves misery, change the company you keep.

You may also find that your friends simply fear your success for their own reasons: they think they will lose you. My single male and female friends were all afraid of losing me when I got married. I had to do a lot of reinforcing to convince them otherwise.

Inventing Your Future

I think you can see that attracting romance will bring you into conflict with yourself, your existing relationships, society, and even your religious beliefs. But if you have the courage to see yourself and your environment as they really are, you can find and fix every weakness.

One of my favorite movies in the world is *The Graduate*. Benjamin graduates from college and doesn't know what he wants to do. He's cloaked in his parent's goals. Mrs. Robinson seduces him and they have an affair. Ben then falls in love with her daughter and overcomes the goal conflict with his parents, her parents, and society to begin his life with Elaine.

You can begin now to work on the internal and external obstacles to your romantic success. And remember that even though these changes spawn some conflict, they will help everyone get what they need in life and help shape the society of the future.

We're all lazy, so don't expect to succeed overnight. We all have reliable ways of avoiding change. Identify and eliminate them. If you don't eliminate your avoidance mechanisms, you'll begin to notice physical symptoms—lethargy and exhaustion. These are all signs that you're not doing what you could be doing with your life. It always seems easier to be lethargic than to know what to do and do it, but the results you achieve are dependent on your intention to succeed. The opposite of avoidance is awareness and awareness leads to success.

Become a reverse paranoic: see every problem as an opportunity to grow and learn. If you repeatedly attract the same kinds of frustrating relationships into your life, ask yourself what you need to learn from these experiences. The only reason you keep repeating them is that you haven't learned the lesson they were meant to teach. If you love like a fire fighter, always starting infernos and then dousing the flames, you may need to learn some creative fire prevention techniques.

People are the bottom line. If you're giving love, but not receiving, it may be because:

1. you don't love yourself enough;
2. you don't believe that you deserve to be loved.

Treat everyone, including yourself, as the most important person in the world. When you recognize the good and love in someone else, your love will be accepted and returned. Remember that a stranger is just a friend you haven't yet met.

As you work on little successes, shifting your viewpoint from failure to success, your self-esteem will blossom and your health will improve. As you overcome your negative emotions—fear, worry, guilt, and hate—you'll begin to love yourself.

In the following chapters, we'll look at ways to make your future come alive!

Chapter Three

Wizards and Magicians

What the great man seeks is in himself.
What the small man seeks is in others.
Confucious

SUCCESS SECRET:
Take responsibility for your life.

MICHAEL JACKSON RESTATED THIS THEME in a recent song: "I'm starting with the man in the mirror." It was hard for me to understand this at first. It really irritated me to be honest, but if we aren't living the life we'd like to be living, if we're struggling in a mediocre relationship or agonizing over finding one, then our actions, beliefs, and thoughts have created our present circumstances. In other words, no one is to blame; our lives are *our responsibility.*

SUCCESS SECRET:
See no evil, hear no evil, think no evil.

The thoughts we think, the things we visualize, the things we believe, and the way we act are working harmoniously to create our life. We are totally, 100% responsible for what goes on in our life, not somebody out there; not our parents; not our spouse or mate; and not the government. You and I. We are totally responsible for what happens in our lives.

Let me give you an example. You've gotten dressed for an evening out. You're wearing something attractive and expensive. You sit down to eat a meal and say to yourself: "I *hope* I *don't spill marinara sauce* on my clothes. I don't have time to change and I'd be embarrassed to wear soiled clothes the rest of the evening."

The word *hope* carries with it both the possibility of success and failure. The phrase *don't spill the marinara sauce* is actually a command to your subconscious to *spill the marinara sauce*. The subconscious overlooks the word *not* and creates a picture of spilled sauce.

So, you've just given yourself a command to spill the sauce and you hope it won't happen. Bingo! You drop a piece of garlic bread in your lap, butter side down and flip a fork of linguini along with it. You can get really mad at yourself and say, "I knew that would happen," or you can calmly call the waitress over and ask for some club soda to take out the stain. By thinking about what can go wrong, you attract the misfortune.

I was in downtown Denver at a soup-and-sandwich place. The guy in front of me, dressed in a charcoal suit and a red tie, said, "I hope I don't drop it," as he picked up a container of soup. As he left the woman behind the counter shook her head, "He comes in here every day and, as often as not, he drops it on the way across the street. I turned to follow her gaze; he crossed the street, tripped over the far curb, and, you guessed it, dropped the soup; it splattered all over the sidewalk and his grey slacks. He had programmed himself for failure.

You buy a new car. You worry yourself sick that someone will nick it or scratch it and sure enough, within a few days, someone taps it. Sometimes you worry about having an accident, and then have one or two in a row.

Sometimes you'll sneeze and say to yourself, "I hope I'm not catching a cold." Twenty-four hours later you're in bed, sick as a dog.

At other times, you may get "the feeling" and buy a lottery ticket; it's a winner. These are simple examples of how we can attract people and experiences into our lives. We are each responsible for what happens every minute of every day and for how we respond to what happens. We can choose to be one of the few who invent our own future, or join the masses that sit around wishing, complaining, and blaming others for their misfortune. Moment after moment we have to find our own way. If we take responsibility for everything that happens to us, we open up the opportunity to create a life that is everything we want it to be.

You cannot suddenly change how you've been doing things all these years, but you can become conscious of what's working and change what isn't. To do this, however, you must look inside yourself and not to others.

Anger comes from blaming others. Stop blaming and your negative emotions will dissolve. Instead of blaming others for your problems, ask:

1. What can I learn from this?
2. What does this reflect about my self-image?
3. What thoughts have I been thinking?
4. What have I been saying to myself?
5. What kinds of images have I been visualizing.
6. What's not perfect about this yet?
7. What can I do now to improve this situation?

There's always a payoff for whatever happens to you. I've had times when I didn't like myself very much, so I attracted people and events to reinforce that belief. I've attracted negative relationships to punish myself for running away from good ones. My self talk and imagery during those occasions was almost always negative. I found that my resentment toward certain relationships always came from having betrayed myself. These women always reinforced what I believed about myself.

On a softer note, don't blame yourself for things that aren't your fault. Forgiveness is the key to all miracles. Forget the past. Do something now, today, to improve your life. Similarly, feel good about being a winner. You have to like yourself a lot to let yourself win all the time. Have you ever felt guilty about having too much fun? If not, you're in the minority.

If you think it's hard to change yourself, just notice how impossible it is to change other people. This is the fallacy of trying to change our partners and co-workers; they won't change unless they want to. How do you get them to change? Change yourself first! Change is inevitable; personal growth is always optional. Get inside your head and ask, "What do I want that would make me feel so good that I couldn't resist improving?" If you get an answer, you'll know you're on the right track. "What do I desire that would make me feel so great that I would leap at the chance to improve?" When you know the answer to this question, you have the fulcrum and lever to move mountains, because you'll have found the heart of what motivates you.

Self-Deprivation

You are deprived of nothing except by your own decisions. If you don't like the relationships you've been attracting, decide otherwise. Change your mind.

We tend to see problems as something outside of ourselves. "That's not my problem. It's John's problem," or "It's Sharon's problem." If you're not part of the solution, however, you're part of the problem. Accept responsibility for turning every problem into an equal or greater opportunity. Chart your own future.

The only fool-proof way to know exactly what we believe and what we're doing to attract relationships into our lives is to look at the results we're getting. If we're getting poor results, we're putting out poor thoughts. For example, "All the men I meet are jerks," will draw jerks into your life in droves. Or a man can say, "I don't know how to meet women," and he'll be right! I used to say that I didn't know how to meet women in bars, but that I was great in elevators, on street corners, almost anywhere else. And I was right! In almost fifteen years of prowling around in nightclubs with friends, I can count the number of women I met in bars and subsequently dated on one hand, and those encounters occurred because my desire for companionship overwhelmed my dominant belief. I wasted a lot of time and money that could have provided me with lots of fun and interesting companions.

Exercise:

Take one belief you have about your lack of romantic success and roast it! Treat it like a 20 lb. bag of manure and instead of carrying it around, spread it over your garden and see what grows. If you don't believe there are any available men or women, spend a day counting all the men or women you see.

There are no shortages of available men and women to meet your needs. The shortages we experience—money, romance, or good jobs—are simply a result of a belief that these things are in short supply.

Loneliness

You can only be lonely when you don't like the person you're with (yourself). What you resist, persists, and what you accept, dissolves. If you resist loneliness rather than accepting it, you will intensify your loneliness. If you accept that you are going to be alone some of the time, your loneliness will vanish. So there are five cures for loneliness:

1. Learn to love yourself. (Chapter 4 - Self-Esteem)

2. Increase the number of friends and people in your life.

3. Make these contacts multiply.

4. Plan for the future. Who would you like to know and what would you like to have one, five and ten years from now? What skills or abilities will you need to accomplish these goals. What can you do right now to learn these skills?

5. Increase your ability to meet people by increasing your ability to communicate —verbally, non-verbally, and on paper. The quality of your life depends on the quality of your communication with others.

   Verbal–Attend the Dale Carnegie Course in Public Speaking and Human Relations. Join Toastmasters.

   Non-verbal–Study body language and Chapter 9 on communication. Learn the science of rapport.

   Written–Writing well will unlock many doors. Love letters and poetry can change your life. Attend a fiction or poetry writing class at the local university.

If you're not learning how to communicate with others, you're going to be one of three things: a victim, a savior, or a dragon.

Victims, Dragons, and Saviors

Victims have the attitude that life is something that happens *to* them. Victims tend to believe that there's nothing they can do to heal their life. Victims often look for dragons to reinforce their life script. Victims may leave a relationship or job before they are left or fired. Saviors, on the other hand, assume the role of the martyr by trying to save the dragon's victims. Saviors can be both hurters and healers; it depends on how you want to be saved!

When we attract a dragon who acts less than lovingly towards us, that person is merely showing us a side of ourselves that we do not love and accept. The major obstacle to resolving our lives is that we deal with problems as if they are something outside of ourselves. Anger and self-hatred attracts dragons who are angry and terribly willing to give the hate and abuse we desire. Happiness and love attract loving, happy people into our lives—people who don't have to save us, just savor us.

Exercise:
On a scale of one to ten, where are you?

1	2	3	4	5	6	7	8	9	10
Self-Hate								Self-Love	

To change these roles, we need to become both a warrior and a magician.

Warriors and Magicians

Warriors take responsibility for their lives. If something's not working, they change it. Warriors take *action* to get what they need. Wizards and magicians use their innate powers and ordinary magic to attract people, places, and things that help them be the best they can be.

In Chapter One, we did an exercise, stating, "I am willing to change!" But in being true to ourselves, we can become uncomfortable. Every time we get that "I'm special" feeling, that stubborn "who do you think you are" question may rob us of feeling good about ourselves. The trick is to ignore that voice or change its tone. Typically, it's not even our voice; it's the voice of a parent or a teacher or someone of authority.

Exercise:
> Listen to the voice that speaks to you inside your mind. Who's voice is it: a parent's, teacher's, or your own? Is it harsh and critical or warm and loving? If there is something you don't like about it, change the voice tone and rate so that it is supporting, loving, caring, guiding, coaching—anything you want.

SUCCESS SECRET:
What you give out, comes back, multiplied.

To succeed as warriors and magicians, we must understand and use the Law of Cause and Effect: As you sow, so shall ye reap!

In other words, whatever we put out, comes back to us, multiplied. If we say, "I'll never meet someone here in the middle of New Jersey!" we won't! We won't even make any friends! (I know, because I spent a year in New Jersey believing this. Once I gave up this belief, wonderful people and circumstances moved into my life.)

SUCCESS SECRET:
Give thanks for what you already have.

If we give thanks for the relationships that we already have, we'll attract more into our lives. You see, by focusing on what we have, as opposed to what we lack, we can magnetize ourselves to attract instead of repel. By giving thanks for the abundance in our lives, we draw more in. Try this now!

Exercise:
> Take as long as you need to give thanks for the relationships you already have in your life—parents, aunts, uncles,

brothers, sisters, friends, whoever. Repeat this often! "I give thanks for _____, who has been a great_____."

And what if we don't have any relationships to be thankful for? Invent some. Pretend that you already have great relationships in your life. Give thanks for the bank teller who smiles at you during a transaction, or the open, caring nature of a waitress at your favorite restaurant. Whatever! Give thanks. It works!

Giving and receiving are two sides of the same coin. What we give, we receive. In a sense, we give only to ourselves. For example, I've heard catty women decry another woman's success in meeting and dating an attractive man. This is poverty thinking at its worst. This criticism returns to them, often in the way that other women and men view them. It's no wonder they can't find a date!

Men do the same thing. Men rate women on a scale of one to ten. "There's a *seven*." "Take a look at that *nine!*" How can men expect women to be attracted to them when they are constantly judging a woman before they've even met her? Aren't men who judge women in fact judging themselves? They can't see themselves with a nine; so they approach someone that more or less matches their own internal scale of self-worth. The most successful men I've ever met refuse to say unkind things about women.

SUCCESS SECRET:
See perfection in everyone you meet.

We can't condemn a man or a woman for succeeding just because they know how to succeed. By choosing to see the perfection in everyone, no matter how tall, fat, short, or beautiful, we free ourselves of the judgments that others reflect back to us. Others will begin to see each of us as perfect human beings.

Giving can only *increase* what you possess. So start giving only love and happiness. See if the people in your life don't suddenly blossom in the light of your gifts.

Become a warrior! Become a magician!

1. Recognize that you are totally responsible for your current situation. You're feeling what you *want* to be feeling.

2. Judge yourself with loving care. Forgive yourself, because you've been doing the best you know how to do at this moment! You haven't lost your ability to learn and improve.

3. Conceive a better life. Ask yourself, "How would I like to feel?" "What do I want?"

4. Use your warrior and magician to build your life.

Once you take responsibility for your life, you'll begin to feel in control of your destiny. You'll find ways to make the choices that will make your life improve. When you begin to follow the path your warrior and magician will create for you, you're on the road to romantic success.

Chapter Four

Claim Your Power

You can claim your personal power by seeking a meaningful direction for your life or by seeking a known goal—companionship, love, marriage, a new job, and so on. To acquire your unlimited power, however, you must:

1. believe in the existence of personal power; and

2. claim it!

To be successful, you need to study success. Reverend Robert Schuller suggests in his excellent book that *Success is Never Ending and Failure is Never Final*. I couldn't agree more. In this chapter we'll look at ways to achieve romantic success.

To attract romance, you will have to help another person get what they want. Remember that we're all looking for the *feeling* we get when we achieve a successful relationship, whether it's a one-night stand or a lasting marriage.

Success is simple! It doesn't require "hard" work. It does require some key steps that I'd like to share with you now. These steps work with romance, other relationships, and even with money.

Follow the Yellow Brick Road

In the *Wizard of OZ*, Dorothy gets back to Kansas by actively pursuing success. Like Dorothy, we can each develop the success habit. Once we acquire this habit, we're more likely to achieve the

Wizard of OZ experience—our lives rapidly zooming from black-and-white into Technicolor.

```
SUCCESS SECRET:
Success is a habit.
```

Failure is also a habit. The way we've been doing things, either positively or negatively, brings us certain results. When we repeat and become comfortable with these behaviors, they become habits. If you're not experiencing the right results in your life, I'd like to share with you ways to get started on the Yellow Brick Road to Success.

```
SUCCESS SECRET:
Success is a process not a place.
```

First, you'll need to start developing the success habit. Success always follows what I call the stairway to success. It's simple. All you have to do is decide to break away from the crowd and walk up the stairway. You cannot jump to the top. You cannot run up it. You have to take one step at a time, go at your own speed, and, in time, reach the top. The stairway to success looks like this:

                                        Achievement
                                 Persistence
                          Action
                    Planning
              Goals
        Permission
Purpose

Success is achieved by the following seven steps:
1. determining the definite major *purpose* of your life;
2. giving yourself *permission* to receive your desires;
3. setting meaningful *goals* that reflect your purpose;
4. developing *plans* to achieve your goals;

5. taking *action* to do what you've planned to do;

6. *persisting* until . . .

7. *you achieve* success.

Have you ever known an attractive, intelligent man or woman who can't seem to succeed at romance? Meanwhile, there are mousy *housefraus* and blue collar men who have the house and family that these "beautiful" people often desire. The beautiful people obviously lack a clear blueprint of their life's purpose, and the goals and plans to achieve it. Oh, they may have a great plan for corporate success, but they usually haven't got a clue about what they want personally. All they need is a purpose, permission, goals, plans, action and persistence. What they focus on must appear!

SUCCESS SECRET:
Success begins with the decision to succeed.

As we discussed in the last chapter, the results you achieve depend on your intention to succeed. If you intend to succeed immediately, you will. The first decision you have to make is to change. Your resolution to succeed is more important than anything else. If you're willing to change your attitude, you can start to change your life immediately.

Define Your Purpose

Each of us has a unique purpose in life. We're not just the odd result of our parent's romantic evenings together. We each have a reason for being here which involves the growth and evolution of the planet and the human race. It may be to be President or a mother or a civil rights leader or a writer. Our work helps us find our identity and our perfect mate. If you're in a job you love, you know how much it can energize your life. If you're in a job you despise, you've at least learned something about what you don't like to do for a living. Try something else.

Exercise:

> In your notebook, list all of your strengths—the things you do well. Then, list what you would most like to do to help other people. Armand Hammer, from the time he was a child, prayed to God to be able to help others. He became a multi-billionaire and his efforts have helped millions of people.

If you find it hard to identify your purpose in life, you're not alone. If you're having a hard time identifying strengths, it's often because you're looking at your weaknesses. If you're not sure that you want to help others, remember that all wealth and love comes from other people. Those who are generous, also prosper! People are the path to personal wealth, happiness, and love.

> *Mastering your destiny and fulfilling your dreams*
> *is the ultimate purpose of life.*
> —Mark Fisher

When I did this exercise, my strengths were *vision* and *creativity*. I want to help you learn to attract romance, and do it far easier than I did. From these strengths and desires, I fashioned the following purpose:

I use my creativity, NLP, writing, and speaking skills to help people learn to (1) do things easily, (2) live better, more enjoyable lives, and (3) develop more unity and oneness.

Use your strengths and desires to create your own purpose in life. This sentence should make you sing with excitement. It should make you feel great. Your purpose can include things you already do well, but a great purpose will cause you to grow! Once you've got a purpose, especially if it conflicts with what Mom and Dad and your friends are telling you to be, then you will need to get permission to achieve that purpose.

Give Yourself Permission

You must give yourself *permission* to succeed. Permission is a ritual that gives you license to change your behavior. I know this sounds silly, but most of us are afraid of success. For a long time I felt that I'd lose my mother's love if I developed a successful relationship and got married. I still felt that way when I got married, but I also gave myself the permission to have the intimacy and love that I need and deserve.

Exercise:

To give yourself permission, write and repeat the following phrase often:

I fully and freely accept wonderful relationships in my life now.

As you begin to operate within the purpose of your life and give yourself permission to succeed, success will come much more easily. You'll go with the natural flow of your life, not swim against it.

Choose Your Goals

Next, you have to *decide exactly* what you want, not what someone else wants or what you've been told you need or want, but what *you* want. These decisions are goals. The world will step aside for the person who knows where he or she is going!

People find their greatest happiness through their work. When we choose a goal and invest ourselves in it to our limits, whatever we do will be enjoyable.
—Dr. Mihaly Csikszentmihalyi

Some people see work as an endless cycle leading nowhere. Without goals, it's easy to see why. Without a clear objective, any path will do. With a clear-cut goal, however, only the appropriate paths can appear. The Puritan work ethic is only half right; with clear goals <u>and</u> hard work, anything is possible. Setting goals and achieving them creates self-esteem (Figure 4.1).

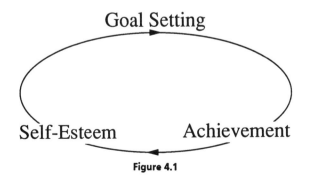

Goal Setting

Self-Esteem   Achievement

Figure 4.1

Trying to start and build relationships will be difficult, only if you don't have a clear, specific goal about what kind of a relationship you want. If you have desire, you can have anything you want, provided you have specific goals and a plan to achieve them. Trusting in fate to deliver the *Wizard of OZ* experience gives you one chance in a million. Trusting your goals gives you every chance in the world.

We've all heard the old saw: "Nature abhors a vacuum," and it is true. If you don't have goals, nature will create some for you; your life will be dominated by someone else's goals.

```
SUCCESS SECRET:
Set your own vivid, life goals.
```

A goal is a vivid mental image or experience of what you want. Your goals determine who and what you will be, and where you are going with your life. Goals push us out of our comfort zone, and growth is life! Discomfort means you are learning and growing. Comfort means you are stagnant, decaying. Don't let nature set your goals; create your own life! If your goals are worthwhile, they are bound to scare you at first, but you must be willing to work for them. As the old saying goes, no one gets out of here alive, so make the most of it. Set your own goals. Strength and energy come from having vivid lifelike images of what you want.

Goals are where you want to go; problems are barriers to getting there. To develop your goals you'll need to:

1. *Set clear, specific goals* (fuzzy ones don't work). For example, a warm, loving relationship isn't specific enough. A friend of mine used this goal and she attracted an ex-husband and a long-standing male friend. A warm, loving relationship with a man/woman with dark hair, medium build, a good career, who dresses stylishly, etc., is a more specific goal. You can have long-range (marriage and family) goals or short-range goals (meet someone and get a date). Your relationship goal must be:

—stated in positive terms.

—something you can initiate and control.

—described in all five senses—smell, taste, touch, sight and hearing. How will you know when you have it? Where, when, and with whom do you want it?

—ecological. How will having this goal affect the other aspects of your life? What will get better? What will get worse?

—appropriately sized—meet someone, get a date, grow the relationship, get married, grow the marriage.
Your goal must do something even more important for you. Meeting someone, for example, may increase your self-esteem. Marriage may provide a loving, stable environment for you to achieve your purpose in life. What will these goals do for you?

2. *Set times* for their achievement. Otherwise, you can postpone them forever. The difference between a wish and a goal is a specific date for its accomplishment.

3. *Write them down*, so that you can review and revise them. The act of writing down your goals will encourage their accomplishment much more than just thinking about them. Tony Robbins says that he wrote a six-page description of the woman he wanted to marry. His wife Becky fit the description perfectly.

4. *Decide the price* you're willing to pay to achieve them. What will you need to give up? What skills and abilities will you need to acquire? Tom Cruise and Bruce Willis, for example, both gave themselves ten years to succeed in acting. Monarchs have given up their throne for the women they love. This is why we ask the *ecology* questions above. What are you willing to do to attract romance now?

5. *Think about your goals* every day. Anything you hold in your mind, you can have.

To be effective, goals must be measurable, life enhancing and as specific as you can make them. In this book, I'll mainly discuss relationship goals, but to be really successful in life, you'll need a balanced set of goals covering your career, finances, and relationship needs, as well as your physical, mental, and spiritual life. Some key questions to answer about your goals are:

Do I really want this?

Am I aware of any problems with this goal?

How will it affect other people?

Why do I want this? What is important about this goal?

Will this goal conflict with any other goals?

How will it help others?

How can I reach my goal?

Where can I get competent information and guidance?

Is it positive, *specific*, realistic?

Is it achievable, believable, and measurable?

What most people don't realize is that they can pay a low or a high price for the same goal. The first price that life asks is always the cheapest. In my own case, I met a great person in high school and we dated through our freshman year in college. Unfortunately, I let real and imagined pressure from parents and friends break us up. My grades slid for four straight semesters until I took control of my life again. Having learned little from that experience, I repeated the behavior off and on over the years.

It's possible to go a long way cloaked in another person's goals. We often travel a long way cloaked in the goals of our parents, our lovers and our employers. It took me a long time to decide that what I really wanted was a supportive marriage. It took me a number of years to decide what kind of a woman I really wanted in my life. But once I decided on exactly what I wanted, it took only a few months to meet my wife, and two years later we were married. The sooner you make these decisions, the sooner you can have what you need and deserve in your life.

Once you've decided what you want, you've got goals, but goals aren't things you can do; they're only places you want to reach that are out there, somewhere, in space and time. You need to develop the *intent*—desire, belief, and acceptance—to follow through. You can test your goals this way—do you truly desire your goal, believe it can happen, and are you willing to accept your goal? If you do, you've got a solid goal.

Build a Plan

Once you've got a purpose and some goals, you'll need a plan. I believe that anything can be accomplished if you break it down into small enough pieces and begin taking action. Failure to plan means planning to fail. If you want to meet someone in a similar occupation in the same city and state, the only planning you need is to schedule time to mix with people. If you want to meet a model in L.A., or a Wall Street tycoon, but you live in Tulsa, you've got to make a much larger plan and break it down into many smaller steps.

Planning starts with the goal you want to achieve and works backwards. Planning identifies the step-by-step actions to get you to your goal. The trick is to start where you want to be and work backwards. For example, to get married you could work backwards as follows:

GOAL	PREVIOUS STEP
married -	engaged
engaged -	in love
in love -	intimate
intimate -	having fun together
having fun together -	getting together
getting together -	ask him/her out
ask him/her out -	meet someone
meet someone -	do what I love to do
do what I love to do -	decide what I love to do

You cannot start from where you are and plan your way to your goal. You must work backwards.

SUCCESS SECRET:
Choose small, meaningful steps.

Within your plan, decide on some first steps that are so small and manageable that you can do them tomorrow. A woman may choose to spend 15 minutes shopping in the Men's section of her favorite department store, or spend some time in a park or a neighborhood bar. A man may choose to spend fifteen minutes in a shopping center, a supermarket, or a neighborhood restaurant where women congregate. Try something new every week. Anyone can do anything for 15 minutes.

Planning, to most people, seems like drudgery and hard work because they don't know how to do it. NLP offers a wonderful way to both experience the goal and determine the steps to achieve it. Most Americans and Europeans have a *time line* on which they store memories of the past, experiences of the present, and expectations of the future (Figure 4.2). By simply imagining this line on the floor, we can walk into our past or our future. For about 80 percent of you reading this book, past and future will be organized as shown. For the remainder of you, it will be organized the opposite way: past on your right, future on your left. There is some evidence that this difference has to do with left- and right-handedness, but there are too many exceptions to make it a rule.

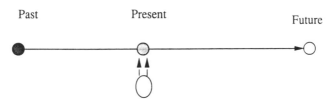

Past   Present   Future

Figure 4.2

Exercise:

Find a long open area and stand in the center (Figure 4.3). Notice that your past, present and future lie along this line. Now step onto the time line facing your future. Walk forward to the point where you know you have achieved your long-term goal for developing romantic success. Notice what you see, hear, feel, smell, and taste. Now turn around and look back toward the present. Now where's your anxiety about achieving your goal? Gone? Good. Notice all the skills and abilities you have now, in the future, that the you back in the present will need to acquire. Send an energy beam of these skills and abilities to the you back in the present.

Now, turn back to face the future, and slowly, one step at a time, step back toward the present. Notice the activities you will need at each step in your plan to enable you to achieve your goal. Only step back when you have a clear sense of what needs to be done at each step. When you return to the present, step off your time line and write down everything you need to do to accomplish your goal.

Once you have a rough draft of your plan, you can use your creativity to invent truly innovative ways to get to your goals. I read a story of a man from Brooklyn University, a student who didn't have much money but wanted to meet attractive, sexually active women, who were also free of social diseases, and amenable to fun, but inexpensive dates.

He took the innovative approach of meeting women in the lobby of a free VD clinic. In the waiting room, he could share openly with the women waiting. His sense of humor often opened up a dialogue about the perils of intimacy. Misery loves company and he was able to make several contacts. He followed up, got to know the women as their treatment continued, and was in a position to know which one was more keenly balanced to his own personality and goals. Then he was able to pursue a more romantic relationship.

Past   Present   Future

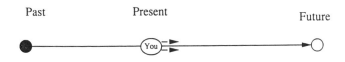

Figure 4.3

These women satisfied all of his criteria: attractive, sexually active, disease free, and, since they were using a free clinic, inexpensive. At first blush, this approach may sound manipulative, but it was actually very successful. And who cares what path we choose, as long as we succeed in creating win-win relationships?

These paths can make life so much more fun. When you're having fun, you won't have any problem taking the next step: *action*. Action turns dreams into reality.

Take Action

> ### SUCCESS SECRET:
> Personal power begins with action.

The next step is to work your plan. Let your warrior run free. Get out and do the things you love. If you like to go to the museum and study Van Gogh, plan to go often! If you like to golf or ski or sail or play racquetball or bounce to the beat of good music in an aerobics class, plan to do it often! Daily action taken toward your goals boosts your self esteem.

You rarely meet the right person if you stay at home. Results only begin to come forth after you start toward them. Most of us have had the experience of meeting someone while we're on vacation in some exotic locale. How did that happen? Easy. We had the desire for a vacation romance and we were relaxed and open to the experience. Openness is more potent than any other system of actions.

You can do the same thing in the comfort of your home town. Go out and enjoy life. When you're relaxed and enjoying everything, the right person will just slide into your life. In between encounters, you'll be having a lot of fun that will make you even more attractive as a person.

Action, however, is the phase that blocks a lot of people. Action often runs you into any one of numerous obstacles. One of the most common obstacles is the fear of face-to-face communication; later chapters will give you the tools—visualization, affirmation, and rapport—to prepare your mind, body, and spirit for those meetings. Right now though, let's look at how to get motivated to meet someone new.

Most people get blocked by thinking about all of the things that can go wrong. NLP has modeled motivation strategies and the best ones don't concern themselves with what you will have to do to meet someone—only the result. A good motivation strategy for meeting someone new would be to:

1. see someone you want to meet;
2. say to yourself,
   "It will be great after I've met that man/woman";
3. imagine what it will be like after you have been talking comfortably and intimately for a while;
4. say to yourself, "Let's do it";
5. start moving toward the person; let nature take its course.

When you do get into face-to-face encounters, remember, there is no failure, only feedback. Every time you try something, you get a response. If you get a date, or just the thrill of having shared some romantic electricity, great! If you get a neutral or "negative" response, recognize it as an opportunity to learn! You can:

1. *Recognize and reward yourself* for acting on your dreams. We'll talk more about rewards later, but give yourself a little something special for taking the risk. It will reinforce your risk-taking and encourage future success.

2. *Decide what you did well* and resolve to keep those skills in your repertoire.

3. *Analyze what didn't work* and change it. Develop more flexibility. Analyze what happened and create three new choices for ways you could have approached the same situation. Imagine how each would have turned out. (See Tape Editing in Appendix B.)

4. *Refuse to criticize yourself.* Criticism, from within or without, will stifle your reaction the next time you decide to meet someone.

SUCCESS SECRET:
Failure is 90% of the distance to success.

Trial and error eventually lead to success. Many people, however, are waiting for something to happen. Ask yourself, have you taken any risks lately? There's no disgrace in giving your best effort. The only real disgrace is in never trying.

SUCCESS SECRET:
You've got to be bad, before you can succeed.

The most common cause of failure is quitting after a temporary defeat. Expect to do badly at first, but be prepared for immediate response. Every mistake is a stepping stone to success. Remember that as long as you practice the exercises in this book, you cannot fail unless you quit. You must have faith that the relationship you desire will appear; you must believe, without any evidence to support it, that something will change.

I tried numerous ways of meeting women until I settled on a way that used my natural abilities—humor and honesty. Interestingly enough, when you use your innate talent, you attract people who are right for you. When you try to be someone you're not, you draw in riff raff from the four corners of the globe.

Exercise:
> On a blank page, write all the skills you can use to build a successful relationship. This can include anything from being understanding to skydiving. Go ahead! List everything! You're a dynamic person. Give yourself some credit. We'll use these clues later to help you craft ways to be in the right place for the right person.

Don't take yourself too seriously. You're out here to have fun. We all possess treasures within ourselves. Vitality comes from expressing the special light within ourselves. Each conscious choice to live at our best reaffirms our self-esteem.

To truly have something we desire, we must first release all attachment to acquiring it. Holding on to what we want only interferes with the flow of energy. Goal setting lets our internal autopilot know where we want to go and what we need when we get there. Letting go is like letting go of the steering wheel in a car or a plane, the autopilot can then resume control and take us to our destination.

Take it easy. Have faith that the right person will appear and it will be easy to meet them. If it's easy, it must be right. If it's hard, you're pushing.

Develop Persistence

SUCCESS SECRET:
Persist until you succeed.

The last trait, persistence, is perhaps the most important. Sylvester Stallone wrote many screenplays before *Rocky*. *Gone with the Wind*, by Margaret Mitchell, was rejected 38 times before it was accepted. A typical salesperson knows that it may take five sales calls to sell a prospective client. No matter how slowly you move at first, persist. In the Bible it says: "Ask and you shall receive." With a formula like that you'd think more people would listen. As Tony Robbins says in his great audio cassette program, *Unlimited Power*, "Notice, I didn't say 'Bitch and you shall receive.'" You must ask and keep asking until you receive. It is only through persistence that we can overcome the obstacles to our success. Be patient as you persist. If you are committed to success, you'll create it. What you desire must appear.

We're always motivated when we really want something. You have the right to grow, be yourself, be loved, self-esteem, self-respect, health, happiness, freedom, and success. Most of us, however, feel that we don't deserve a perfect relationship. Because of this belief, most people will go through the following three stages when using this book:

1. I'm not sure I can do this.

2. This isn't working. Things are getting worse!
   I want to quit.

3. I'm going to do it until I succeed!

It's *always* too soon to quit. Believe in yourself even when everyone else doesn't. If you believe, no one else will matter. Remember, the way you are living now is a habit. You are used to being single or married or alone or whatever. Changing these habits will push you out of your comfort zone. A little discomfort means you're growing. A lot of discomfort means you're pushing too hard. Ease up.

Achievement

This process of giving yourself permission to succeed, deciding on your goals, planning for their completion, and taking action will lead to the fulfillment of your needs and desires. You will find, as you move up the stairway to success, that you will need to change your goals, plans, actions, and reinforce your *intent*. This is okay! After all, it is your life and your future. Change is the natural state of all matter in the universe.

What traits do you need to develop or change to ensure romantic success? Here is my list:

1. **Passion** - a burning desire to achieve the relationship you deserve.

2. **Belief** - that you can have what you desire.

3. **Strategy** - the step-by-step "stairway to success" for achieving your goals.

4. **Clarity of values** - a belief in win-win relationships. You can get what you want by helping others get what they want. Never compromise your integrity, morals, or faith.

5. **Enthusiasm** - the energy to carry out the actions necessary to achieve your goals.

6. **Communication** - the ability to mentally, emotionally, and physically bond with people.

7. **Persistence** - the ability to keep learning and adjusting your plans and actions until you achieve your goals.

Recognize and reward yourself every time you do an exercise from this book, get out and mingle with people, or take a chance. There have been times in my life when I felt invincible. I could walk into a party or a bar where I knew almost no one and talk and dance with any woman there. There are other times when I got rejected time after time. Often, instead of saying to myself: "YEAH! You took a chance. You tried. Great try!" I'd replay the woman's reaction and think that I just wasn't good enough.

Focus on what you want to grow in your life and reward yourself whenever you get even a little of what you want. If you reward yourself for every attempt to meet someone, you'll soon become fearless and successful. If you focus on failure, you'll attract failure and a shattered self-esteem. Every night in a bar, every encounter at Dairy Queen for an ice cream fix, and every chance meeting in an elevator teaches us something. Relive your successes often and learn from them. Replay your failures only once, write down what you've learned in your notebook, and then throw that experience in the trash.

```
SUCCESS SECRET:
Improve yourself constantly.
```

What else can you do to encourage your success?

1. Decide to build a burning desire to create a dazzling romance.

2. Read inspiring, uplifting books to reinforce your positive emotions and reduce the power of your negative emotions. I've listed some of my favorites in the resource section at the end of this book.

3. Listen to cassette tapes. The average person spends 2,400 hours a year in a car. Cassette tapes will help you constructively use the time you spend in your car every day.

4. Read one book a month on a subject you find interesting or useful on your job. Almost 70% of adults never read another book after they leave high school or college. One book a month will put you in the top 5% of all people in the country in three to five years, and in the top 5% of the world in five to seven years.

5. Choose and develop positive new friends and relationships in areas other than your romantic interests. We all need balance in our lives. Nothing is more dangerous than a relationship when it's the only one you have.

Be yourself, do what you love, and you will get what you really want. As Goethe said, "What you can do or dream you can, begin it! Boldness has genius, power and magic in it!"

In the following chapters, I'll show you how to develop the genius, power and magic that lies dormant in your mind. May the force be with you.

74

Chapter Five

What You See is What You Get

IMAGINATION IS ONE OF THE KEYS to attracting romance. This chapter's title strikes me now as a perfect way to express the importance of seeing and experiencing people, places, events and things in our imagination as a precursor to having them appear in our lives.

Walt Disney used his imagination to delight millions of people the world over. The studio coined a term for turning imagination into reality—imagineering. I'd like to help you learn to be an imagineer. The first step is to learn to visualize your goals. Whatever you visualize, even if it doesn't exist in your life now, will materialize. So, in a sense, what you see is what you get.

On a similar note, Napolean Hill said: "What the mind can conceive and believe, the mind can achieve." People from Missouri, the "Show Me" state, tend to say, "I'll believe it, when I see it." Unfortunately, they've got it all backwards. As Dr. Wayne Dyer says it: "You'll see it, *when* you believe it!" When you can see, hear, and truly feel how you want your life to be, you'll see it manifest in your life quickly. Your life will turn out the way you see it turning out.

Most people believe that life just happens to them. There are a host of bumper stickers that reflect people's beliefs:

Stuff happens!   Life's a bitch and then you die.
                    Live fast, die young.

Bad things don't just happen. First we have to eat ugly thoughts and pictures, digest them in our subconscious (which attracts these thoughts and pictures into our lives), and *then* bad things happen.

SUCCESS SECRET:
Your mind cannot distinguish between
real and vividly imagined reality.

Your internal goal-seeking mechanism cannot tell the difference between reality and vivid, imagined scenes. If you can imagine the life and lovers you want to have, in sufficient detail, your goal-seeking mechanism will attract them to you; there are no exceptions.

Unfortunately, many people waste their imagination on worry and disaster. They worry about the worst possible thing that could happen. Then, bad things happen. Or they waste their time thinking about how much effort will be involved or how long it will take to accomplish their goals, and then they procrastinate and never get started. Our vision of our *self* establishes our behavior. It can cause us to act unloving, obnoxious, or aloof. It can cause us to sabotage our success, or drink too much, or fail too easily. Getting a clear picture of what you want is essential to making yourself aware of your opportunities to enjoy the life and love you deserve.

As you learn to visualize, you will discover that you cannot travel within and stand still without. If a woman visualizes herself as attractive to the type of men she wants to meet, she'll change weight, her style of dress, or whatever she needs to do to attract the kind of man she wants to meet. Men will find themselves shedding their stiff masculine demeanor in favor of a more sensitive, open approach.

SUCCESS SECRET:
Prelive your future.

To attract romance, it is essential to prelive the future, not relive the past, especially the negative failures of the past. It's easy to get caught up in reviewing failed relationships and past experiences. This will only attract more of the same. You need to learn to preview the experiences you *want* in your life.

To see yourself succeeding in attracting romance, you'll need to determine your personal strategy for "seeing" the future.

Visual, Auditory, and Kinesthetic

The programming language of the brain consists of images, feelings, and dialogue, all of which can be enhanced or dulled by various submodalities (Table 5.1). You don't necessarily have to see your goal; you can hear it as words, or just feel it. Of course your goal will appear more quickly when you imagine a total experience including all three—pictures, sounds, and feelings. As we'll see in a later chapter, there are three main communication styles: visual, auditory, and kinesthetic. These people may say things like:

Visual–I *see* what you mean. That *looks* good to me.

Auditory–I *hear* what you're saying. That *clicks* for me.

Kinesthetic–That *feels* good to me. I'm *warming* up to that idea.

Whichever is your dominant strategy—visual, auditory, or kinesthetic—feel free to "visualize" your desired goal in all its glory, using your specific approach; then add in the other details. For example, as you begin *feeling* what it would be like to be with the man or woman of your dreams, notice how they are dressed and how they *look* physically. Also begin to notice that you can *hear* what he or she sounds like and what they would be saying to you. Crank up the vivid clarity of their appearance, the texture of their skin, or the sound of their voice to make them irresistibly attractive. This was vividly illustrated in the movie, *A Fish Called Wanda*. Jamie Lee Curtis portrays a thief who is instantly turned on by men speaking in foreign tongues—Italian, Russian, or Spanish. Having had an English girlfriend, I can confess to a certain pleasure from hearing her melodic, English voice. Southern women, with that smooth, sensual drawl, can turn a man's head as easily as a Bostonian can turn a woman's. Part of John F. Kennedy's appeal was his eloquent accent.

Table 5.1
Submodalities

Representational System (Sense)	Submodalities
Visual (Seeing)	Brightness
	Clarity or haziness, fuzziness
	Color/black & white
	Color balance or hue
	Contrast
	Distance from the image
	Foreground/background
	Frame around picture or panorama
	Focus
	Location (up, down, center, right, or left)
	Motion (movie, slide, or photograph)
	Perspective (looking down upon, up at, bird's eye view)
	Seeing yourself in the picture
	Seeing everything with your own eyes
	Size (large or small)
	Shape
	Sparkle
	3-dimensional or flat, 2-dimensional
	Vividness
Auditory (Hearing)	Clarity
	Continuity
	Distance
	External or internal
	Fullness (a live performance or just a cheap recording)
	Location
	Monaural or stereo
	Number of voices or sounds
	Pitch
	Rhythm
	Tempo or speed
	Timbre or tonality (rich and full, or weak and frail)
	Volume
	Words or sounds
Kinesthetic (Feelings)	Intensity (hot, burning, cold, freezing)
	Movement (from one place to another)
	Location
	Pressure
	Scope (how large or small of an area)
	Temperature
	Texture
Smell	Aroma

```
SUCCESS SECRET:
Use all of your senses to create
a future that excites you.
```

Richard Bandler says that if you aren't licking your lips in anticipation, then your image of the future still isn't compelling enough. Adjust any of the "submodalities" in Table 5.1, until you get an image of the future that is so exciting that you feel drawn toward it.

Creative Visualization

Each of us has a synthetic and a creative imagination. The synthetic imagination pulls together pictures stored in our minds and creates new images. The creative imagination simply invents scenes in our minds. The creative process is a by-product of our sexual energy. Enjoy it.

Olympic athletes use visualization to preplan their entire performance. Having recently taken up golf, I find this an important tool to help bring down my score. When I clearly visualize the ball landing in the fairway, on the green, and going in the cup, it does! All great golfers do this. Salesmen use visualization to imagine their customers getting what they want, and the intense feeling the salesmen will get when customers buy.

Before you approach a man or woman, or before you call someone on the phone, take a few seconds to visualize this person responding favorably to your call or advances. It will double your chances for success. Visualization is essential to romantic success.

The steps of creative visualization are:

1. Get a clear picture of your goal.

2. Imagine the end result. Feel it! Hear it!

3. Clarify your desire. How much do you want this?

4. See yourself in the picture. Add action, emotion, sight, sound, smell, taste, and touch.

5. Repeat these four steps often. Strength can only be developed through repetition and effort (Figure 5.2). The more you rehearse your experiences, the greater your chance for success.

6. Lock out conflicting images.

7. Give thanks *as if* what you want has already appeared.

Power Programming

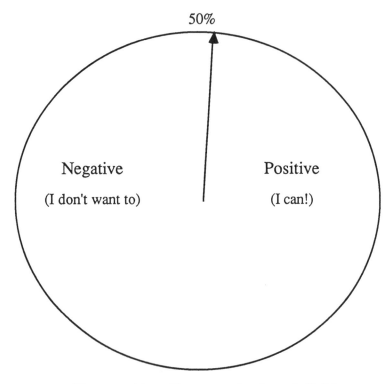

How repetition affects your dominant beliefs!

Figure 5.2

As mentioned earlier, some people may have trouble "seeing." If you have trouble visualizing things, it may have to do with where you are looking at that moment. For most of the population, pictures most easily can be remembered and created by looking up and to the left or right. If you watch visual people, you'll often see them looking up to remember or synthesize pictures in their mind. Auditory people will look to the left or right to remember and create sounds. Kinesthetic people will look down to remember feelings.

Earlier I mentioned Walt Disney. This creative man's personality had three aspects (Figure 5.3)—the dreamer, the realist, and the critic (Dilts 1990). The dreamer created vivid images of how the animated film would look. Of course, images with action remain nothing more than dreams; Walt had a realist that laid out the plans for creating the movie and actually drove most of the production. There are many stories of ideas and products that never made it in the real world; Walt had an internal critic or "spoiler" that evaluated both the *dream* and the *plan*. Using the critic's analysis, the dreamer and the realist would then tune up the vision and the actions required until Walt's internal critic was satisfied. We all know the result of these cyclic actions: some of the best loved animation ever created.

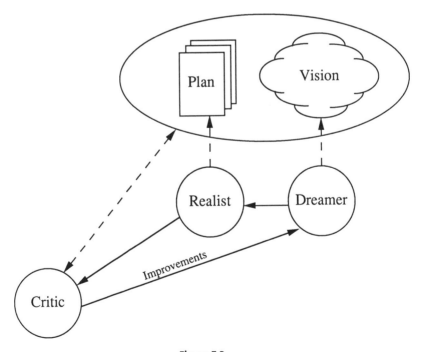

Figure 5.3

Use creative visualization and link it to action. You'll begin to see changes in your behavior. Visualization produces results. Persist!

For example, in 1985, I'd recently gotten out of a long, but unsatisfying relationship. I decided that what I really wanted was a happy, supportive, satisfying marriage. I followed these steps:

1. I imagined myself as married, not single anymore. (This was not easy.)

2. I got a clear picture of how I would feel, curled up at night with my wife. My love strategy is very kinesthetic. I envisioned how we'd relate the rest of the time. I also imagined that she would have children, because I wanted the experience of fatherhood, but didn't necessarily want to go through the whole pregnancy-to-college process.

3. I knew that I wanted a marriage that supported my writing, personal growth, commitment to travel and financial success. I wanted someone I could help and who could help me. A woman with children who owned her own house and had her own career seemed to fit the bill.

4. I saw us being comfortable in foreign countries, at home, and at the movies.

5. I held this vision clearly and steadily. Women started to flood into my life. As I learned more about what I did and did not want, I changed my picture. About four months after I started, my wife appeared in my life for the second time. The Universe had introduced us about five years before, but we didn't listen. In 1981, she was recently divorced and I couldn't see myself with a woman with two daughters. Remember, you can always pay the cheapest price first. We struggled for almost five years before we came back together.

6. I locked out the image of my mother's disapproval. I knew my father would love whoever I found.

7. As this all worked, I bonded easily to my wife. It took longer for her to come around to the idea that marriage was a viable, desirable solution. I've discovered that most divorced women with children have decided that they'll never marry again or

that no one would want them (because of their children) or that they never want to be hurt again. As long as they believe this, it's true. Remember, we create our experiences, so we often choose our first mate poorly and attract painful divorces to reinforce our personal beliefs.

What did I do in the face of my wife's opposition? Persist!

I should note, however, that visualization will work only when it helps *everyone* get what they need. You cannot violate another person's will by asking for them specifically. You can't visualize yourself into a relationship with someone if it would hurt them or someone else. For example, you can't visualize a man or a woman out of a marriage, unless it's in the best interests of both husband and wife. Visualization won't work if:

1. you're not convinced that it will.

2. you're too lazy or skeptical to try.

3. you don't really desire what you visualize!

4. you're violating someone's personal will.

You can't always get exactly what you want, but you will always get everything you need.

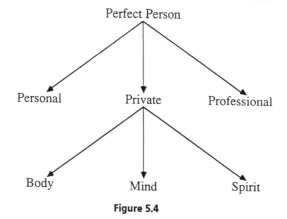

SUCCESS SECRET:
The Perfect Person Exercise (Figure 5.4)

Perfect Person

Personal   Private   Professional

Body   Mind   Spirit

Figure 5.4

Exercise

Write a complete resume of the person you would like to meet. Choose the *type* of person that seems the most exciting to you, even if he or she seems the most inaccessible. Cover everything: height, weight, hair, eyes, looks, body style, how they dress, education, hobbies, sports, activities, political affiliation, sexual prowess, vocal tone, how much money they make, where they live, etc. Do you want to be married, just have fun, or enjoy intense sex? In these perilous times, include "disease-free" as a criterion. Be as specific as possible; your subconscious can only produce results from a clear mental image. At the bottom of the page write: "This or someone better manifests in my life now for the good of all concerned!"

If you have trouble defining what you want in a lover, write down what you don't want first. Then take each undesirable quality and write down its positive alternative. Instead of, "I don't want someone who smokes," say instead that, "My perfect lover never smokes."

On the opposite page from the description of your perfect lover, paste a picture from a magazine of someone that most resembles the person you would like to meet. This visual guide is often referred to as a treasure map. It will help you *see* the type of person you want to meet. This was demonstrated in the movie *Romancing the Stone*. Joan Wilder has a poster in her office of the faceless man she wants to meet. She is drawn to Colombia to meet him. Avoid becoming obsessed with meeting a particular celebrity or person. Visualization only works for the resolution of everyone's needs. Unless you are a celebrity or have a plan to become one, you are probably setting yourself up to fail. Why would you want to do that?

If you have trouble with resumes, you might try making a perfect lover wheel (Figure 5.5). Start in the center with the word *lover, husband, wife, girlfriend,* or *boyfriend*. From this word, draw radiating lines like spokes on a wheel to key qualities you want this person to have. Draw further spokes off of each of these words. Add pictures to the wheel to represent each of these key qualities and a central picture to represent the person.

Perfect Lover Wheel

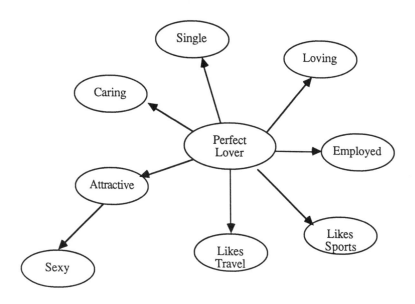

Figure 5.5

I call this the *perfect person* exercise. By establishing a clear visual and mental image of the person you would most like to meet, you are 90% of the way to meeting that person. To achieve your goal, reread the resume daily and use the photographs to refresh your subconscious picture of the perfect person. Repetition is the key to imprinting this person into your goal-seeking mechanism. When you've finished rereading the resume, close your eyes and experience what it would be like now to enjoy this person's company. *Feel* what you would be feeling; *hear* what you would be hearing; *see* what you would be seeing. Let this experience wrap you in a golden glow.

The more emotion and detail you can put into the picture, the more quickly this person will appear in your life. Once you are clear about what you want, others will be able to respond.

Review this resume and treasure map daily. Vividly imagine what you want and repeat, repeat, repeat. Change your internal image and your internal guidance system will make your goals reality.

Some of the people who've tried this exercise have told me that it helps with existing relationships as well. Most of the time you know you're going crazy in a relationship, but you don't know why. With your perfect person defined, however, you'll know why your current mate isn't working and what you need to do to enhance or replace your relationship.

Exercise

Create your ideal day. Imagine what your life would be like with this perfect person. Step out into the future six months, one year, and five years from right now and imagine what your life together will be like. Imagine where you work and what you do for a living, where you live, and how you live. Create a treasure map to support these desired goals as well. (You might as well use these tools on your whole life.)

As you visualize the future, how do you feel? See your body. How have you cared for it? How do you dress? Where's your perfect home? What does it look like? What's your perfect work?

Use Disney's realist and critic to build a path to these desires.

To encourage the acceptance of these futures, review them before you go to sleep each night and in the morning after waking. You can also review these exercises at times other than before or after sleeping, but you will need to relax first. To do so, take a long, slow, deep breath, hold it for a count of five, and, as you exhale, count slowly from ten to one. Do this three to five times and then picture your goal exactly the way you want it. You can do this at the office during a break.

SUCCESS SECRET:
Repetition is the key to imprinting your goals.

The unconscious responds to the dominant thoughts in your mind. Use visualization often. Repetition is the key to developing, experiencing, and imprinting your goals in your subconscious mind. You don't have to repeat your goals all by yourself. You can call on others for help in this area as well.

Exercise

Write the names of five people, living or dead, whom you respect and would like as mentors to help you develop relationships. Relax deeply by breathing and counting backwards from ten to one, and then imagine yourself in a quiet place in nature. Imagine that these five people are with you, around a table or a fire. Ask them what advice they can give you about succeeding in romantic relationships. They will answer. Write down their advice and review it often.

Visualization will give you one of the three key tools to ensure romantic success. To enhance your visualization, you can also use dreaming.

Dreaming

Sometimes dreams are wiser than waking.
—Black Elk

Most of us spend one-third of our lives asleep. Most of us have remarked how much we could accomplish if we didn't have to sleep so much. Well, you *can* use that time. Dreams, if you use them correctly, are one of the most powerful success tools you have. Freud called dreams "the royal road to the unconscious." Dreams fuel desire.

As you drift off to sleep each evening, you've already visualized your romantic goals. This sets the stage for supportive dreaming. If you've been wondering what else you can do to increase your chances, you can tap your dreams for this information.

Exercise

As you start to nod off, say to yourself either aloud or in thought: "I want to dream of ways to attract and improve the quantity and quality of satisfying, romantic relationships in my life. I also want to remember the dream when I awaken in the morning." Keep a pad of paper by the bed to write down your dreams when you wake up. Write them down *in bed*. I find that if I don't capture them immediately, I can lose them just by getting out of bed and taking a shower. (The subconscious dreamer disconnects as the rational mind takes over.)

Study what you learn. What can you do now to enhance your chances?

There are two types of dreams: realistic and symbolic. In America, most dreams are symbolic. Dreams thrive on metaphors. The nocturnal theater of the mind contains a mother lode of symbols. Symbolic dreams can be interpreted through a dream dictionary, or you can make your own interpretations by writing the symbols down and asking your other-than-conscious mind what they mean. Realistic dreams, on the other hand, are often prophetic.

I was a junior in high school; I wasn't dating anyone, but I liked one of the women in our class. She was already dating another guy and I thought the case was hopeless. Then I had the dream. I dreamed that a bunch of students went up to Mount Lemmon—a 6,000 foot peak outside of Tucson, in the middle of winter. There were 20 of us in a huge dormitory-like barn. We played in the snow. My dream woman was with the guy she was seeing and I was solo. Later, however, when evening came, she and I were alone in a small cabin. The door was open and it was a warm, spring evening. We were in bed together. My mother walked through the door and tucked us in.

In the spring of that year, her relationship ended and we dated through the summer. My mother never approved, but you can't have everything. This was a highly prophetic dream. Most of mine are symbolic.

One more thing you can use is lucid dreaming. Dreams typically continue the conscious concerns of wakeful life, but in the dream language of visual metaphors. In a lucid dream, you become conscious and control the outcome of the dream. Ten percent of the population has the ability to do this naturally. All you have to do is recognize that you are creating the dream so you can also step in and change your dream. If figures or beasts pursue you, you can turn on them, shoot them with a gun, or become huge and drive them off. If you are having a dream about someone you want to be involved with, you can change it to match your goals and desires. I'm not saying this is easy initially, but you create your dreams, so you have the ability to adjust them to meet your needs. Just do it.

Between dreams and visualization you have two powerful tools to enhance your romantic life. Use them! Next we'll look at the second success tool—thinking—and the way thoughts impact your ability to attract romance into your life now.

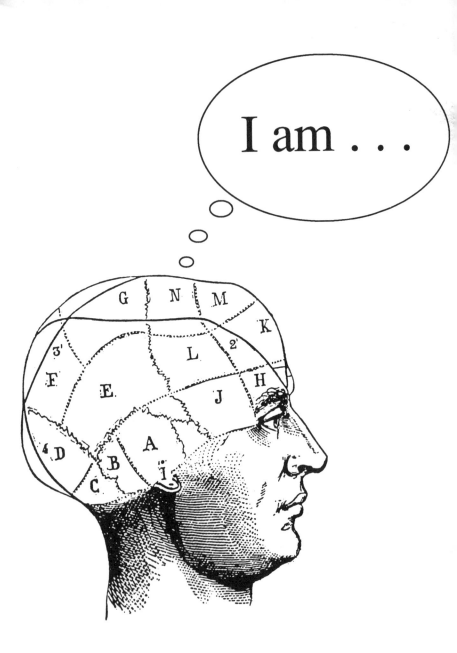

Chapter Six

I Think, Therefore I Am

Thinking is the hardest work there is!
—Henry Ford

> **SUCCESS SECRET:**
> There are no "idle thoughts."

Each of us has over 50,000 thoughts a day. Repetition of these thoughts has created your past and present, and they are creating your future. Every thought of the past has created your present. Whether you are rich or poor, sick or healthy, lonely or fulfilled, your thoughts have played a key role in creating your present, and they are creating your future.

In the Bible, it says, "As a man thinketh within himself, so is he." (Proverbs 23:7) Our thoughts produce results all the time. If we don't like the results we're getting, we need to change our thoughts. If we are wracked by thoughts of limitation and self doubt, we develop a mind set that interferes with our ability to attract romance.

Some people say, "It's hard to meet people these days," and they're right. They attract people and circumstances into their lives that affirm what they are telling themselves. Other people say to themselves, "Everyone plays games; no one is ever honest and open." And you know what? Even if honest, loving people came into their lives, they would see the world as a playing field and treat these people as players.

I've had times where I would think, 'She wouldn't be interested in me,' but I'd talk to a woman anyway. My subsequent aborted approach, lack of enthusiasm, and general demeanor would telegraph my beliefs: 'You aren't interested in me, *are you?*'

Of course, she wasn't. This question presupposes that she wouldn't be interested.

And I've had the opposite experience. I describe the experience as feeling *hot*, so hot, in fact, that I hear the sizzle like water dropped on a hot griddle. Walking down the 16th Street Mall in Denver, feeling great about the day and myself, women will look at me and smile as I glide through the crowds at lunch hour. I'm usually thinking in a supremely confident tone and volume of voice that 'I feel good! I feel great!' and it shows.

If you tell yourself you can or you can't, you're right.

Exercise
Every day for a week, get up every morning
and say to yourself:
I feel good! I feel great! Someone wonderful
is going to happen to me today!

You may find this so exciting that you'll want to do it indefinitely. It helps your attitude about work and everything you do. You'll still have some bad days, but they'll be fewer and farther between.

SUCCESS SECRET:
Your thoughts think you!

This last exercise will begin to prove to you that you don't think your thoughts; your thoughts think you! A beautiful mind yields a beautiful body. Your thoughts create you—that extra fat around the thighs or waist, your success at the office, how much money you make, and the level of love and romance in your life. To change your results, focus your thoughts on how you want life to be, not how it is.

> ### SUCCESS SECRET:
> Whatever you think about expands.

There's a place inside of you where nothing is impossible. By directing your thoughts, you can further improve your life. You can become your own imagineer. I want you to think about love, romance, abundance, financial prosperity, and any other need in your life.

You are magnetic. Your thoughts attract whatever you think about. If you're getting bad results, change your thoughts right now.

He who cannot change the very fabric of his thought will never be able to change reality.
—Anwar Sadat

Exercise:

List your thoughts for 60 seconds or so. Are they the kind of thoughts you want shaping your future? Are they positive, negative, or neutral? Reshape the negatives into positives.

If you find a thought that you don't like, say to yourself, mentally, 'Cancel, cancel,' then say a strong, positive thought three times. For example, some of us sneeze and think, 'I hope I'm not catching a cold,' but because we thought about it, we do. (The mind doesn't hear the word *not*. So all it hears is "I hope I'm catching a cold!") When you catch an unhealthy thought, shout in your mind, "STOP!" and say, "Cancel, cancel. I feel good! I feel great! Perfect health is mine now!" A woman I know caught a cold every time she went home to see her family in Michigan; she flew home often because she was connected to one of the airlines. She had a habit of saying, "I always catch a cold when I return from Michigan," and she always did. I told her to stop programming her mind that way. Since she started programming her mind with perfect health, she hasn't had another cold.

The same is true of relationships. "I'll never meet anyone. There's nobody out there for me. Nobody loves me, everybody hates me, guess I'll go eat some worms."

This kind of negative programming is holding you back.

Exercise

Every day for a week, catch every negative thought you have about relationships and say to yourself, 'Cancel, cancel. The perfect man/woman appears in my life now!' And they will.

All you have to do to begin changing the results you're getting in your life is to change your thoughts. Everyone is free to change their mind and all their thoughts with it. The old wives' tale says that changing your mind is a female prerogative, but men shouldn't let that stand in their way. There is nothing that a change of mind cannot effect. All external things are only shadows of mind-thoughts already pondered. When you change these mind-vapors, how can their shadows remain unchanged? Remember, the only reason you don't have someone in your life is because you don't want them badly enough!

Beliefs

Our existing beliefs, either negative or positive, focus the life force of the universe that flows through us and creates our life. Our thoughts act like a magnifying glass focusing the sun's rays; they focus our life force into power for both good and bad. At every moment in time, our minds are evaluating and thinking about everything going on around us. We evaluate everything against our values and beliefs. Each of us has a vested interest in our current beliefs. In fact, most of us believe that we will die if we lose our dominant beliefs.

SUCCESS SECRET:
Beliefs can be changed.

Change your beliefs and you will change your life. That's why I asked you in the first chapter to affirm: "I am willing to change." Beliefs come from our environment, experiences, knowledge, and past results. Almost all of us have beliefs from our parents, teachers, and past lovers or husbands or wives. All families are dysfunctional in some way. If you grew up with alcoholism, divorce, physical or sexual abuse, I urge you to seek professional counseling to clear any personal roadblocks you may have to success. Even if your family was more traditional, you may have roadblocks to success. Some of us believe that no one loves us, or that we don't deserve love or that loving can only hurt us. These are all ways of punishing ourselves. When we learn to love ourselves, these beliefs will disappear.

Exercise

List five positive beliefs that can empower you to find and build meaningful relationships. List five negative beliefs that keep you from enjoying the level of happiness and love you deserve.

I used to say that there were three perfect women for me, but they all live in South Dakota. How would I ever meet them? I also used to believe that the best women were married. Any guesses about what happened? You got it; I attracted many married women into my life. Since college there have been at least a dozen. Some were friends, some were lovers.

But, if your goal is a satisfying, supportive marriage, there's a problem with seeing married men or women: their divorce and your marriage is rarely a win-win solution. For you to end up with someone else's spouse, each person must benefit from the dissolution of the marriage. This is rarely the case. The person you're seeing feels guilty about breaking up the marriage. The spouse or children are often hurt in the process. It's a win-lose situation in 99% of all extramarital affairs, and the Universe only supports win-win situations.

I decided, as you can if you're involved in an affair, that you no longer desire these kinds of relationships. You can begin to tell yourself, as I did, that there are thousands of great single men and women out there just waiting to share a warm, loving win-win relationship.

If you don't decide this about extra-marital affairs, then you are punishing yourself. You will have trouble developing the relationship you deserve until you change your beliefs to support your success. Every successful person, whether in relationships or the stock market, shares some key beliefs:

1. Everything happens for a reason or a purpose, and, regardless of what happens, it can be made to serve you and your success.

2. There is no such thing as failure, only feedback. You can learn from every experience: good, bad, or otherwise. If one thing doesn't work, try another and another. Persist!

3. Whatever happens, take responsibility, because your beliefs and thoughts and actions created the situation.

4. People are your greatest resource. Form a success-oriented team to help you get what you want.

5. Work is play. Finding and building excellent relationships should be fun, not pain. If you're working too hard to find a relationship or to make one work, it's time to try a different tactic.

6. No one can succeed without commitment and desire. You don't need beauty, brawn or brains if you have these two.

With these beliefs—and I suggest you review them often—the only shortage of romance you can experience is the result of a belief. The only foolproof way to know what we believe is to look at the results we are achieving. If you can't tell what's going on from looking at the results you're getting, ask your dreams. You will get an answer.

Let's Talk

We have two forms of communication: internal and external. How we communicate with our romantic interests determines part of our success; but how we communicate with ourselves—our self-talk—helps set the foundation for our success.

When you do talk to yourself, you can change the location, volume, and tone of voice you use to be supportive and encouraging. Add stimulating music. Add a chorus of background singers to support your actions. As Richard Bandler would say, "Even Elvis did that." When you need to be critical, criticize your *behaviors*, not your *self*. Use "tape editing" or the "new behavior generator" (Appendix B) to create at least three new behaviors to substitute for the old one. Give your *self* a break. As you practice attracting romance, you will learn things that you can use as motivation to improve some aspect of your personality.

Also, remove the opportunity for others to criticize your desires. As you read and practice from this book, I recommend that you tell no one. Everytime you ask for someone's approval, you put a rope around your neck. What *other people* think of you, your ideas, and what you're doing to improve your life, is none of *your* business. Their negative thoughts can cloud your progress. I've had discouraging words from more than one friend, lover, or relative put me in a purple funk for days over writing projects.

The subconscious mind—our goal-seeking system—does not respond to wishes, but it will respond to clear visual images and positive thoughts, desires, plans, and persistence. Tell no one about your goals, or tell only the people you really trust. Then see which ones you can really depend on for support and encouragement.

The Irresistible Law of Attraction

> **SUCCESS SECRET:**
> Our dominant thoughts attract!

Our dominant thoughts attract the people, places, events, and forces of life which we require. We can attract accidents and illnesses as easily as we can attract riches and love and happiness. Whatever you believe, you attract. If you dwell on what you do not have, you attract scarcity; so focus on what you *want!* When we think something will be difficult, it is. When we fear something, it is *more likely* to happen.

I took the train from New Jersey into New York City one morning. Sitting across from me was a pale, thin man with nervous hands and black hair. He started telling me about how he'd been mugged three times in the past year. He pulled out his brand new wallet to show me, fluttering his hands like a lab rat on cocaine. He made me so nervous that *I wanted to mug him!* I was glad when he got off in

Newark. Do you think he was reliving those muggings in his mind and thoughts? He had to be.

When you anchor thoughts with emotions—fear, anger, faith, love, or sex—you create a powerful magnet to attract it to you. If you fear being attacked, you may attract it to you! If you have faith that love will appear in your life, it will.

```
SUCCESS SECRET:
The brain does what it's told.
```

In the same way, if we focus on the times we've been 'dumped' or divorced or rejected and repeat those experiences again and again, we draw more of the same to us. When you believe you can have the type of man or woman you idealize, he or she will appear. The brain does what it's told. It makes no difference whether you give your mind good or bad instructions. It doesn't matter where the programming comes from—television, friends, relatives, or co-workers; your dominant thoughts will create your present and future. It's not easy to change, but it is essential to leading an excellent life. Thoughts are the key.

Good Thought, Bad Thought

We all have positive, neutral, and negative thoughts. They march through our minds like high school bands—loud and brassy. Interestingly enough, we are born with positive and neutral thoughts; we learn negative thinking and poverty consciousness from other people. The thoughtless are doomed to be prisoners of other people's thoughts. Prosperity consciousness comes from programming your own mind.

Make no mistake, the mind is a computer—a vast, highly evolved one, but a computer all the same. You can choose to program your own mind or let some hacker on the universal network dump a bunch of defective programming into your mind. And, much like real computer programs, much of this free mind-ware has embedded viruses that can cause diseases and mental illness. Robert Dilts calls them "thought viruses." Take charge of your own programming. At least when you put in a defect, you'll know where to take it out.

Mind Poverty

Ninety-nine percent of our thinking is self-centered. Somewhere, most of us picked up some mind-ware that suggests that there are two types of people: the *haves* and the *have nots*. We simply fall into one of these two categories and that's that. This implies that we can't do anything about our lack or abundance.

Nonsense. When we change our thoughts, we change our future.

SUCCESS SECRET:
Positive thoughts are high-octane superfuel.

Negative thoughts are poison. Poverty consciousness comes from negative thinking. Up to 75% of our early programming was negative: 'Don't do that. Don't try that. Stay out of there,' and so on. All of this negative programming about not taking risks, not getting into things, and not learning how to live life at its fullest is learned from other people. Kids really understand how to live! Unfortunately, the hardest negative thoughts we acquire come from a few key impossibility thinkers—our family and friends. The most common weakness of all men and women is the habit of leaving their mind open to the negative influences of others. Most people's minds are like a beach after a storm, littered with thoughts that wash up from the depths.

Exercise

The next time you get a negative thought, listen to its tone and volume. Is it close or far away? Whose voice is it—father, mother, teacher, yours? Where is it located? Behind one ear or another? Higher up or lower down? Change its power over you. Turn down its volume and push the voice farther away, perhaps behind you. Change it to sound like Mickey Mouse. Have the voice squeak from your big toe.

Think of your own subconscious mind as a child that may have been battered by negative thoughts. Recognize that everyone is, by nature, lazy, indifferent and susceptible to all of the suggestions that mirror or harmonize with their own weaknesses. Guard your mind from the thoughts of others. Like castles of old, put a moat around your mind and a guard at the bridge. Then think of beauty, think of health, think of love. Think yourself young!

Mental Wealth

To achieve the love and fulfillment you deserve, you may have to clean your mind, get the cobwebs and dust out of the corners, oil up the love machinery, and re-energize the beast. (In computer companies, they call this preventive maintenance. It's often done once a month for minor work and at least once a year for major work. I suggest you do the same.)

Thinking about abundance attracts abundance. Giving thanks for all the handsome men and women in your life will attract more. Believing that the perfect person will appear for you now will help make it happen. Any thought or emotion can be changed to a more positive one by looking at it differently; reverse the thought! If you think there aren't enough men to go around (and therefore someone has to lose for you to win), say to yourself, 'There are more than enough men/women to go around.'

Be grateful for the weeds you find in your mind; plow them under for fertilizer. The way you've been thinking is a habit. Having thoughts that don't support your desires is neither good nor bad, but wouldn't you rather have a mind filled with thoughts of pleasure, success, happiness, and fulfillment? Pull in new thoughts and redecorate. Push out the darker thoughts and donate them to Ill Will.

Exercise

There's a little voice inside your mind that repeats all kinds of messages it has learned. Instead of the voice of authority, change its tone to sound like Donald or Daffy Duck. Change the tone so that it makes you laugh. Or change the tone to be low, sexy, and seductive. Now how do you feel about those messages?

If you heard, in your mind, a police officer's voice say, "You can't do that!" in response to an urge you had to try something new, change it! Hear a strong, sexy voice saying, "You can't do that!" This should change your motivation to do whatever you've been resisting.

Now, capture these thoughts in your notebook and turn them into more positive thoughts that you can use to displace the old, outdated ones.

SUCCESS SECRET:
Thought laced with emotion demands action.

Ralph Waldo Emerson said, "The ancestor of every action is a thought." You can increase the power of your positive thoughts by giving them the voice of authority and adding feeling or emotion to each one. Your thoughts will change more quickly. The greater the intention behind a thought, the greater the change in your results. As your thoughts and beliefs change, your attitudes about attracting romance will change, and people will begin to flow into your life.

Sex is the greatest driving emotion in the universe. Sex has always been coupled with creative ability. Sex and love give you poise, purpose, and balance. Sex, love, and romance give you genius. Use sex, love, and romance to anchor the thoughts you want to see manifest in your life.

Think of yourself and others as prosperous, loved, held, touched, whatever. Give thanks for the success of friends and family. Every time you see a happy couple, say to yourself, 'That's for me!'

Look at every day as a challenge and an opportunity to create a successful relationship. Above all, repeat these newfound, positive messages in your mind as you weed out the negative. As you do, the second of your powerful imagineering tools—thought—will go to work to achieve your goals.

In the next chapter, we'll look at the third tool for positive change: affirmation. I'll show you how to use affirmations to override your negative programming and change your beliefs even faster.

Chapter Seven

Cast it in Concrete

Y OUR SUBCONSCIOUS MIND IS NEUTRAL. It operates on the information it's given regardless of the accuracy, content, or value. The subconscious holds no beliefs or biases other than its own programming. Whatever we do, regardless of why we think we're doing it, we're following the dominant programming in our subconscious mind (Figure 7.1). This internal autopilot operates at all times on the dominant program playing in our minds, just like a program in a computer. Our subconscious maintains our body and mind precisely the way that we see, hear, feel, and think ourselves to be. These old programs or habits lock out new options for personal growth. We can, however, reprogram our minds with new habits and attitudes. When faced with two or more conflicting programs, the subconscious will play and act upon the one that's best for us. That's why it may take time for thoughts, visualization, and affirmation to take hold and change our world.

We interpret all experience in terms of our existing programming. We only see what we want to see, hear what we want to hear, and feel what we want to feel. Through simple ignorance of how to program our mind, we allow our lives to be directed by the unexamined programs that we've cobbled together over a lifetime!

We resist change, not because we don't want to change, but because the new programming conflicts with our old dominant thoughts. The old programming is too heavy to be forced aside when we push. That's why it may take time and several attempts to quit smoking or to release excess weight; the internal programming often refuses to be changed overnight. Our self-image must change first!

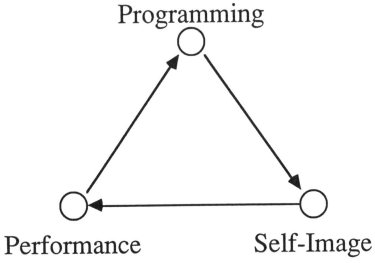

Programming

Performance   Self-Image

Figure 7.1

That's why it takes time to attract the right relationship; our old programming has us locked in a pattern that is preventing our romantic success.

The human mind is not exactly like a computer, however; we can't just pull out the old program and plug in the new. We can reprogram our minds, but we each have only one programmer who sleeps and eats and works another job most of the time. It will take time to get our subconscious reprogrammed to do our bidding. *Affirmations* are another key to changing the programming that is controlling our lives today.

Self Management

Written and spoken affirmations are the strong, personal, positive thoughts that we use to reprogram our minds to achieve the goals that we desire. If we aren't in charge of programming our mind, then someone else—a spouse, a friend, advertising, or our boss—is managing our future, or mortgaging our future more likely.

When you begin to manage your own programming, you will begin to see how much more successful your life can become, not only in relationships, but with your career and life in general. With the right coaching, you may surprise yourself, or your *self* may start surprising you.

Whether you know it or not, you've been using affirmations to shape your future all of your life. As we discussed in the last chapter, the thoughts that run through your mind a hundred times a day are affirming, either positively or negatively, your future. "It's tough to meet people nowadays." Ever heard that statement play in your jukebox? I know I have. How about: "Thank God it's Friday!"

These affirmations are called "self-talk," and the only way to overcome the negative messages is to install a stronger program to replace them. If you dwell on past thoughts, like playing oldies on the jukebox, you can only repeat the past. Do you want to continue to repeat the past or would you prefer to create your future in your own best interests?

If you're in a relationship that's headed downhill or you haven't had a date in some time, are you affirming the problem, "This relationship is history," or are you affirming the solution, "My relationship improves every day"? Are you telling yourself, "I can't get a date to save my soul," or are you talking about the solution, "Men/women love my company"?

Self Programming

> ### SUCCESS SECRET:
> Positive thinking is the natural language of success!

To attract romance, you must learn to work *with* the natural processes of the brain—the subconscious mind. Written and spoken affirmations are part of the programming language of the brain.

Reprogram your jukebox so that it plays new age instead of acid rock, reggae instead of the blues, or classical instead of salsa.

Repetition is the *only way to reprogram your mind for success!* Your subconscious mind will accept and act on anything you tell it, if you present the idea, thought, or picture often and strongly enough. Eventually, conscious thoughts will drop into unconscious awareness and become part of your mental programming. Affirmations give you another success programming tool.

Intent—desire, belief, and acceptance of the relationships—comes from repetition of commands to the mind. Affirmation programming changes your beliefs, which change your attitudes, which change your behavior, which change your actions, which, in turn, change the results you see in your life. The better the program, the better the results.

Affirmation

You can use affirmations in many ways. The more ways you use them, the stronger the program and the stronger the result. You can use affirmations in meditation—spoken either aloud or to yourself in a mirror—written on paper, or with others present.

Affirmations should be positive, personal, present tense, passionate, short, realistic, and should presuppose your success:

1. They must be *positive* - "I am a great lover," instead of, "I'm not a bad lover." The mind ignores the word *not* and hears only, "I am a bad lover."

2. They must be *personal* - "Jay is a loving, caring man." Use your name often.

3. They must be in the *present tense*, as if you already have what you desire. "I radiate love and women/men flock to support me." If you say, "I wish," or, "I want," that puts your request in the *future*. If you say, "I radiated love and people flocked to support me," it puts your success in the past. Either past or future presupposes that you don't have the ability NOW! The subconscious only operates on *present* reality.

4. They must be *passionate*. They must use strong emotive, action words: "I *radiate* love!" "Love fills my life now!" Words that trigger emotions and vivid images will change your programming more rapidly than passive words. There is one exception: the phrase, "I am," is especially powerful. It affirms your identity, divinity, and membership in life. "I am a caring and compassionate companion."

5. They must be *short* so that you can say them, write them, read them, and think them quickly. Take note of advertising 'affirmations' (Coke Is It; Just Do It): the shorter the message, the greater the effect.

6. Affirmations must be *realistic*. They must feel right for you, yet bring up some resistance. You can't affirm, for example, that you are a great lover if you cannot see yourself that way. You are better off to affirm that you are a great kisser. Chip away at pieces of a major problem and the larger problem will eventually dissolve.

7. They must *presuppose* success. "I am in a wonderful loving relationship," presupposes that you have already accomplished your goal. "I easily and effortlessly meet people every day," presupposes that it is easy and effortless. Give yourself a break; presuppose that you will succeed easily and effortlessly.

Affirmations must be supportive. Accept yourself as you are. Give thanks for the abilities you have now, but use affirmations to state how you want to be in the future, now. Change your "I can't" programming to "I can" programming. Say things like: "I give my love easily and effortlessly." "I meet people easily and effortlessly!"

Use affirmations to create a sense of belief that you can have the best relationship in the world. "I have a wonderful supportive relationship." If you've ever had that experience, you know how it feels, so recall the magic. It will reinforce your affirmations.

When using affirmations, realize that you can only affirm for yourself. You cannot affirm for other people, even though, "Men always talk to Stacey!!!!" always seems to work. Stacey is already affirming this; your comments have no impact.

If you say, "Men always hurt me," change that affirmation to, "Men always want the best for me!" If you say, "No woman would go out with me," say instead, "Women love my company!"

The strength of an affirmation is affected by three things:

1. The number of times you repeat it.
2. The amount of emotion/action attached to it.
3. The source of the affirmation; who says it.

A bland affirmation will need many repetitions to insure its installation in the subconscious. A negative thought, however, can happen hundreds of times a day, preventing change from occurring. That's why you need to enhance the emotional impact of the affirmation. The degree of emotion and action you can pack into an affirmation affects its completion:

"I radiate my affection to the Universe!"

The word, *radiate*, gives action and a visual effect to the statement. Compare this with the affirmation, "I am affectionate."

Make your affirmations strong! Sing them to a Jamaican beat and dance as you repeat them. Do anything your subconscious offers to increase their effectiveness.

The source of a program is critical to its dominance. "Nobody will want you! You're poison." These affirmations and thousands like them often come from people we most respect and admire—family. Teachers and police and bosses and peers throw in their opinions and our subconscious accepts them as fact.

Exercise

Check your past for beliefs you've acquired from disreputable sources. Change them with positive programming of your own.

Imprinting

To get a new thought or program entrenched in your subconscious, you'll need repetition, emotion, and action. You'll also need to work on the affirmation in several different ways to stimulate all of your mind:

1. Read the affirmation.
2. Write the affirmation.

3. Visualize the end result.

4. Feel the emotion you'll feel when what you are affirming has become reality.

If we just read an affirmation, it is only 10% effective. If we read and write the affirmation, it's effectiveness rises to 30%. If we read and picture an affirmation, we achieve 50% effectiveness. Combining all three—reading, writing, and visualizing an affirmation, we can achieve 100% effectiveness. This will quickly change the programming in our subconscious mind and bring about the results we desire.

To get the best results:

1. Work on only one or two affirmations at a time.

2. *Read* each affirmation.

3. *Write* each affirmation five times in each of three ways:
   I radiate love to the world!
   You radiate love to the world!
   Jay radiates love to the world!
   You may find negative thoughts surfacing as you write ("I don't want to love anyone, let alone the whole world!"). Write these thoughts down next to the affirmation; this will help remove your negative thought patterns and bring about swifter change.

4. *Visualize* the end result of each affirmation as if it already exists and feel what it would feel like to have that now.

5. *Repeat* each affirmation until it weaves its way into your beliefs. You'll know when your results change; you'll no longer dredge up any negative thoughts. Then your subconscious can be programmed without any interference.

6. *Say* them aloud to a mirror or to another person.

Affirmations—spoken, written, and visual—will reprogram your mind both consciously and unconsciously.

Exercise
This exercise, if you do it, is worth the price of this book. Every morning, rewrite your romantic goals and perfect person exercise. Then, feel what you would be feeling, see

yourself enjoying the achievement of your goals, and hear what you would be hearing. Remember to breathe as you do this exercise. Results will come quickly!

Cement Factories of the Mind

Affirmations make your desires firm. If you think you know what you want but aren't willing to write it down and say it aloud, who are you kidding? You're only using ten percent of your reprogramming ability.

Write your goals. Say your goals aloud to yourself in the mirror. See, feel, hear. Only when your objective is clear (i.e., written) and sensory specific can it manifest in your life.

I started writing and affirming my goals in September, 1988, and opportunities quickly rolled in from places I never expected. *Mental* affirmations have brought me love and jobs and free vacations, but it took years for them to appear in my life. With written affirmations, however, it only takes a few weeks, at most a few months, for success to enter our lives. If you want to succeed at attracting romance, use your three imagineering tools—visualization, thought, and affirmation—to reprogram your subconscious mind. Then all you need to do is relax and trust that the Universe will bring your goals or something better into your life soon.

And it will!

Chapter Eight

The Hero's Journey

Each OF US, ON OUR LIFE'S ADVENTURE, can choose to learn as much as we can and to be the best that we can be. The hero's journey fleshes out our soul, our personality. Relationships are a part of every journey. The hero's journey typically involves three key players: the hero; the villain; and the victim.

In a typical heroic story, an often unwilling hero is forced by circumstance to defeat the villain and save the victim. In *Star Wars*, for example, Luke Skywalker (reluctant hero) battles Darth Vader and the Empire (villain) to save the rebel alliance (victim). Almost every novel or movie involves some sort of hero's journey.

Often, we are our own villain, victim, and hero. We victimize ourselves and only our inner hero can reform our inner villain and save us. We are usually unwilling heroes; we want someone else to save us.

To succeed and grow, we must take charge of our own life. We can refuse to remain a victim by deciding to change our thoughts. We can choose to live deliberately. This is the hero's journey.

The traditional hero, a *warrior*, is a strong man or woman who conquers every barrier to success. Yet this is not the only hero stereotype. There are also innocents, orphans, martyrs, wanderers, and magicians. In *Star Wars*, Luke Skywalker begins as an innocent/orphan. Through his journey, he metamorphoses into a magician—someone who understands and uses the Force. Each of us has one or more of these personalities operating in our lives, one more dominant than the rest. In this book, we've looked at the skills of the magician—visualization, thought, and affirmation—and, like me, you may find that you have other lessons to learn before you can take advantage of these skills to their fullest.

Let's take a look at each of these heroic personalities. See which one best describes your own heroic journey.

Innocent

Innocents are very trusting, too trusting. They believe that everything in the universe exists to serve and please them. The innocent male believes that women are here to care for, support, and please him. The innocent woman believes that men were created to protect and provide for her.

When I first graduated from college, I started in business at—as Henry Miller described it—the Cosmodemonic Telephone and Telegraph Company. I innocently believed that the business of business was to make the customer and shareholders extremely happy. I thought that if I worked smart and worked hard that I'd get raises and promotions commensurate with my effort. Office politics (the villain) showed me that some people were only interested in what the company could do for them, not what they could do for the company. My innocence was slaughtered on the alter of greed.

Orphan

The *orphan* seeks safety and security, but cannot find them. Orphans want the world handed to them on a silver platter, and they are annoyed when their needs are not immediately gratified. Orphans are easily victimized, and they tend to blame others for their lack of safety, lack of a job, lack of love, and lack of life. Orphans will purposefully mess up a relationship to punish themselves. The orphan often feels powerless and remains so unless he or she decides to change.

I have a friend who is a classic orphan. She gets herself fired from jobs and victimized by men. She uses every avenue possible to prevent herself from establishing the security she requires. Rather than take responsibility for her own future, she says it's just bad luck.

Gloria Steinem started as an orphan. Her parents divorced when she was eleven. Her mother's mental illness worsened and Gloria had to care for both of them. "I was encouraged to think that I couldn't save myself; I'd have to marry someone who could." Then she began to take risks and discovered that ". . . if you do something that the people care about, the people will take care of you."

Martyrs

Martyrs are self-sacrificing. Women often fall into this role. Like the orphan, they are easily victimized, but they *seek* the pain and hurt. It cleanses them and fulfills them. Martyrs believe that their existence depends on hard work and suffering. People martyr themselves for companies, parents, spouses and children. Unfortunately, you can't help others until you've healed yourself.

Casanova's women were drawn to his urgency, obsessive behavior, and sexual virtuosity. Most martyrs fall to this sort of courtship without reservation.

Wanderers

The *wanderer* explores himself or herself and every new horizon. This is often a solitary, lonely trip. The wanderer believes that he or she must do it alone. Divorced men and women often assume this role. Wanderers evolve from orphans and martyrs who are finally forced to flee the villain in their lives. This escape launches their personal quest.

The last summer of my college days, I went to Europe with a friend, the first of many wandering journeys. When I left home the following summer, I embarked on a journey that took me to Denver and then across the U.S. to New Jersey and back again. I traveled to the Caribbean and Mexico, Hong Kong and Hawaii, Boston and San Francisco. I also started on numerous personal journeys. I shared some of the stable times with women and then the urge to wander carried me away again. It wasn't until I began to discover myself and my abilities that I stopped looking "out there" for answers and started looking within.

Wanderers, however, must travel before they can become magicians. As we learn through our travels, we grow to the point where we can begin to see our strengths. These are the lessons that wanderers must learn before they can evolve.

Warrior

The warrior's way is twofold: pen and sword.
—Musashi

Warriors are assertive and aggressive. Their quest is one of completion, triumph, and conquering fear. Warriors develop confidence by taking more control of their lives. As often as not, men are pushed into the warrior role in early childhood.

The goal of life, however, is not to win, but to learn. Anyone locked in the warrior role, whether a corporate executive or soldier, may wake up one day and refuse to fight. In *Catch-22*, the bombardier, Yossarian, chooses not to fly. He learns that flying bombing missions in World War II is insane. Once he learns this, he can no longer be a warrior. He must change.

Over the years, I've dated numerous women warriors. Since the 1960's, there has been a phenomenal rise in women traveling the warrior's path. Most have found it mentally satisfying, but emotionally unrewarding. What we all seek is a balance; focusing on one role model or another can only bring imbalance.

A lot of men still operate from the warrior mentality. Women occasionally tell me, "Men in bars are jerks," and this isn't surprising. The most assertive men in bars are either warriors or orphans masquerading as warriors. The magicians are there; they just aren't coming on like a forty-ton locomotive. My suggestion is to look around the hunk of lounge lizard in front of you and look for the man who's gently trying to catch your eye; then you'll know you've found a magician.

Magicians

I remember, as a child, watching the Ed Sullivan show and seeing magicians perform. I've seen magicians use their illusions to change a Siberian Tiger into a beautiful woman. The magicians I discuss in this book are not masters of illusion; they are true magicians.

Any sufficiently advanced technology is
indistinguishable from magic.
—Arthur C. Clarke

Magicians accept pain, fear, loneliness, and powerlessness as part of the fabric of life. They strive to be complete and authentic. Magicians understand that nothing is ever lost. Letting go of the old makes room for growth and life. The magician, like Luke Skywalker, moves with the energy of the universe. He or she attracts what is needed by the laws of synchronicity. Synchronicity, by the way, is what Carl Jung described as "meaningful coincidences." By knowing what they want, magicians recognize opportunities and use these "meaningful coincidences."

Like Darth Vader, however, the magician's tools must not be misused. Without the desire to use the magician's power for others as well as yourself, the magician's power can turn against you. If you look for the negative in life, you'll find it, often to your own detriment.

In my life I've also had the privilege of dating a couple of women magicians—women who were dedicated to living life to its fullest, women who could manifest wonderful success in their careers and other aspects of their life. They felt no guilt about this either! They were willing and ready to receive the magic elixir of life. You can become, as they are, magical!

The Part-That-Knows And The Part-That-Drags

Each of us has two parts: one that drags and one that knows. When someone asks you to *try* something new, possibly something you've never tried before, you may experience the part-that-drags. It makes excuses; it gets mad; it runs for the door. The part-that-drags may be very useful when someone tries to involve you in a shaky business deal, and not so useful when you want to meet someone.

The part-that-knows is connected to the energy and knowledge of the Universe. Have you ever had an experience where someone connects two ideas that you've never thought about before and the part-that-knows says: "Yes, I know." The part-that-knows understands your purpose in life and will help you if you let it.

The innocent and the orphan expect others to save them. Given a chance to save themselves with ordinary magic, the part-that-drags will throw a fit. The part-that-knows will watch this childish outburst and then, when it subsides, say: "Yes, I know that's what we need to do."

The martyr doesn't want to be saved. The wanderer will often overlook the obvious, simple tools of ordinary magic in his/her travels. The warrior may ignore these tools and choose instead a shield and a spear, all because of the part-that-drags. The magician's tools seemed too easy to me, too simple. My martyr wanted to work hard and sacrifice to succeed. My wanderer wanted to search for some romantic ideal. By accident, I managed to use the magician's tools to attract my wife. (Actually I was ready to move into my apprenticeship as an everyday magician.)

Don't let your innocent, orphan, martyr, wanderer, or warrior stand in the way of realizing your power. You may, however, travel through each of the "archetypes" often in a lifetime, but each successive journey will be easier. The magician's art will smooth your path. Begin now to learn the wizard's skills and draw the best of life to you.

Metamorphosis

To change and grow, we must each take a risk and move out of our comfort zones, beyond our current role. Without risk, each of us can stagnate, feeling numb, alienated, empty, and alone. Dare to step out of your existing role, whether innocent, orphan, martyr, wanderer, or warrior. Embrace the magician's art. Use the ordinary magic described in this book to attract perfect relationships into your life.

Like a furry caterpillar, we can all evolve into a beautiful butterfly.

If you want success, trust the Universe to deliver. It will. Each of us chooses the world we live in. Give up the rigid ideas you have about what the world *should be* like and love *what it is*. As you learn to accept the world as it is instead of fighting it, you gain energy and vitality. Your purpose in life will become clearer and more compelling. When we try to fight or rebel, we lose sight of what we want and with that we lose the energy to go and get it.

Fighting the natural flow—the Tao—of life occurs when we think of ourselves as different, alone, and separated from the world as a whole. Rene Descartes was the first to offer the theory of the separation of mind and body. This has been the underlying principle of modern medicine. Doctors are discovering, however, that the mind has a significant impact on the health in our bodies, and devotees of Neuro-Linguistic Programming (NLP) have found definite correlations between our physical and mental states. Similarly, for years now, there's been a running argument about the "war between the sexes"; each side suggesting that if there was something wrong in their lives, it was the fault of the other sex.

Let's stop this bickering. Men and women need each other to learn about their underdeveloped female and male aspects. Neither side really understands the other, but if we would take the time to listen and learn, there would be a lot less tension in the world. As I've said before, to get the relationship that you want, you're going to have to learn how to give other people what they want. If you invest in your education, relationships will blossom in your life like wildflowers in the spring.

Have Faith

Have faith that, when you're ready, the Universe will provide a wonderful new romance. In *The Teachings of Don Juan*, Don Juan explains this faith to Carlos Castaneda as "leaping into the void." You just have to trust that perfection will appear in your life in perfect ways. Faith harnesses Infinite Intelligence, the force that connects all living things, to bring bounty and love into your life. First, you must believe.

Then, you must be patient. You cannot have what you want, unless it exists and is available. There is a waiting period; for some people it's an afternoon and for others it may take months. In the meanwhile, release attachment to your desire. Continue to visualize, think, and affirm what you want. If it is in your best interests to have the man or woman you're requesting, then they will appear as soon as they are available. Sometimes, they have to get out of a relationship to make room to get into yours. If you continue visualizing and affirming but get no results, turn the problem over to the Universe. Miracles happen when you just let go. The Universe will then be free to bring someone even better into your life—someone who will align you with your highest purpose in life.

Alignment

Our lives are like cars! The front end can get out of alignment. We've all seen cars going down the street sideways, wearing out tires every few thousand miles. We can do the same thing to our minds and bodies by not loving ourselves and by affirming outcomes that are not in our best interests. A simple example is saying things like, "The best men/women are married." This draws us into relationships that can't work out.

SUCCESS SECRET:
Study your alignment with your purpose in life.

The Puritan work ethic taught that work was "hard." We've all heard people say life is "hard" and it is if you aren't in alignment with your purpose in life. Instead of taking resistance as a sign that we should do anything else, most people respond by working harder and harder, which puts us farther out of alignment.

There are two basic signals of alignment to look for:

1. **Comfort** - things happen easily. We're filled with energy and enthusiasm for each new day. We must be in aligment with our purpose in life!

2. **Discomfort** - things are difficult, problems keep coming up; we keep repeating unpleasant behaviors and unfulfilling relationships. We keep expending a lot of effort to keep going; we feel exhausted from "efforting."

When we experience comfort and an ease of life that nourishes us, we are aligned with the Universe and using its energy. When we are uncomfortable and using a lot of effort, we are using our personal energy in *opposition* to the Universe. This tires us out. This causes what is known as "burnout." Getting burned out, being fired, or quitting a job or a relationship is a "threshold" experience. At these points we can step over the threshold and begin to create the life we want or sink deeper into despair.

In the movie, *Baby Boom*, Diane Keaton is a corporate superstar who inherits a baby daughter from a distant relative in England. Diane's character eventually moves to Vermont where, using her natural abilities, she develops a line of custom baby foods that take the nation by storm. This is a classic example of how the Universe will force a change in our lives when we need one.

Exercise

Look at your life—job, relationships, personal, private, and professional aspects. Where are you "efforting" and where are you going with the flow? Anywhere you are efforting, ask your dreams for guidance. Ask and demand solutions to the problems facing you.

If you're in a relationship that requires effort to maintain, a relationship that you complain about to your friends, a relationship that just won't get any better but won't get any worse, GET OUT. Make room for good to come in. Stop being an orphan clinging to security. Step into the void and trust the Universe to provide.

Any time you feel threatened or angry or irritated, it's because you aren't living in alignment with the flow of life. Learn to let the anger pass and then ask, "What am I doing to feel this way?" "What can I learn from this?"

Be suspicious of complicated things. When things fall into place, you're in tune with the world. A woman once told me, "Things end up pretty much the way they begin." Good relationships begin effortlessly. They begin in alignment. Questionable ones start hard and rarely get any better.

Radiate your desires and goals and then have faith. The Universe will take care of the details of how and where you will meet your perfect person. Just follow your intuition.

As you wait, avoid impatience. Be aware. The Universe never misses a chance to encourage you. If you're aware of these signals, you can function with total certainty all of the time.

> *Peace is easily maintained,*
> *and trouble is easily overcome before it starts.*
> *Deal with it before it happens.*
> *Set things in order before there is confusion.*
> —Lao Tzu

The Universe offers small hints when you are off track. Small problems can become big ones if you ignore them. If you accept every problem as a chance to learn and grow, you will make rapid progress on your heroic journey. When something goes wrong, it's easy to say, "Why me?" Look inside for the answer. The thoughts you've been thinking and the things you've been visualizing and saying to yourself have brought this about. All experiences are lessons that God would have us learn. Just be open. Ask: "What can I learn from this?"

In a sense, the world is a mirror. What you see is a reflection of your inner comfort or discomfort. Think of the people and animals that love you as a mirror. How do they respond to you? What do they say? What does your job say about your self-worth and sense of alignment? What does your car say about you? Is it clean and well kept, or cluttered and dirty?

Intuition

SUCCESS SECRET:
Good luck is essential to success.

Good luck comes from listening to your intuition!

Your intuition is the compass of your destiny. If it says, "Go to a movie," then by all means go do it. If it says, "Read the personal ads in the newspaper," do it. Suzuki said, "Look at the frog; if something annoys him, he'll make a face; if a fly comes along, he'll eat it." Be like the frog; do what seems right at the moment. Your intuition will guide you to the perfect point in time to meet that special someone.

Some people say, "If you're good, you don't need luck!" Don't believe it. Most people fail because they deny the role of luck in their lives. Luck runs in streaks, either good or bad. Your intuition can help you find the best luck. I have a friend who used to lament, "It's either feast or famine. Sometimes you can't fight them off and sometimes you can't even buy a date." If you learn how to use your intuition, however, the feasts will be longer and the famines shorter.

Intuition is the immediate knowing of something that you could not possibly know. Your rational mind can only tap the knowledge it's learned in your life thus far, but your intuition is your main link to Infinite Intelligence which connects everyone and everything. Most scientists and inventors will tell you that intuition played a big part in some of their major discoveries. Einstein imagined traveling on a beam of light before developing the law of relativity. The remarkable progress of science and medicine in the last century seems to imply that we're on the verge of recombining science with the magician's art. This will lead to an incredible advancement in the quality of life as we know it.

The sixth sense is as precious as gold. Intuition is everything. It can warn us of danger and notify us of opportunities in time to embrace them. Mastery of the intuition requires a clear intention to do so. Intent, again, consists of desire, belief, and acceptance.

There are a few steps to developing the intuitive powers:

1. Realize that intuition is a spiritual facility.
2. Act on your intuition, especially for small things.
3. Act on your desires.
4. Prepare for some surprises.

Your intuition is always correct, but it takes time to learn how to listen. To master intuition, we must release our conscious, rational, analytical mind in favor of our intuition. When I was in college, a friend and I decided one year to go to California for Spring Break. I immediately began to feel bad about the decision, but I wanted to go so badly that I ignored my intuition. We had planned to go in my friend's car; he wrecked it a week before the trip. We flew to Los Angeles and stayed with his relatives. I came down with a temperature of 103 degrees and lost 25 pounds in seven days. His relatives started leaving us at home so we 'borrowed' his cousin's car; it broke down and I had to fix it. They threw us out and I had to call a friend to come get us. Anything that could go wrong did go wrong. On the other hand, my intuition has guided me into student cafeterias, ski lodges, bookstores, and various places where I've met truly interesting women.

The best advice I have is trust, trust, trust your intuition.

Exercise
> As you commute to work, instead of perhaps getting angry with the traffic, use your intuition to choose lanes and paths that will ease your progress. Imagine you're choosing one lane or another before you do it; do you feel positive or negative about the choice? Follow your intuition for a week. Notice what happens!

There are some excellent books on developing intuition, which I've included in the Resource section. All you really have to do is listen to your intuition, and act on what it tells you. If you trust it, magic will happen in your life, almost on a daily basis.

Trusting your instincts is another way of loving yourself, because you align with the Universe and begin to use its energy to make your life more magical.

Foundation

If this is your first exposure to these concepts, you'll be a little skeptical. That's okay. I was skeptical at first, but you must suspend your disbelief long enough to experience them. Soon you'll be forming loving relationships in every aspect of your life.

Build a support group. Work with other men or women to share the experiences you want to attract into your life. Share methods of improving your intuition. Two heads are better than one. Napolean

Hill calls any group of two or more people a "Master Mind." The power to manifest success in your life is equal to the square of the number of people in your group. So two people have the power of four; three people the power of nine, and so on. Other people can help you see what you cannot.

Trust the Universe! Step into the void! Let your intuition guide you on your hero's journey. Don't be afraid to act; it's just the part-that-drags holding you back. Follow the part-that-knows. Trust yourself; you hold the key to your own power, future, and success.

Chapter Nine

The Communication Challenge

T ONY ROBBINS SAYS THAT THE QUALITY OF YOUR LIFE is the quality of your communication, with yourself and with others. Now that we've talked about internal communication—visualization, thought, and affirmation—let's talk about external communication; how do we develop rapport with the man or woman we want to meet?

SUCCESS SECRET:
Deal with others in *their* terms.

The answer is simple. You can help others most by learning to deal with them from their communication style.

The meaning of your communication is *the response you get.* We've all had the experience of meeting someone and having instant rapport. As we talk, we think, 'he or she is just like me.' How does this magic happen? It's easy, we all have ways of dealing with the world. When we find someone who has similar ways of managing his/her life, we feel instant rapport. Their body language, the way they talk—the words they use, the tonality of voice and rate of speech tell us that we're the same. Like attracts like, opposites repel.

Similarly, we've all had the experience of meeting someone and being completely at odds with them. These people seem diametrically opposed to us. How can they think that way? It's easy; they think, see, and feel in different ways. They run their brain in different ways. Other people always respond to *their* map of reality, not yours. They *are* different, but we can learn to enter their world and communicate with them. They are also the people from whom we have the most to learn *because* they are so different. If you want new choices and more flexibility, you can learn most easily by modeling people who are different than you.

Personality Types

Although there are many personality types, one useful model is shown in Figure 9.1. In this chapter, we'll explore the four personality types—driver, extrovert, analytical, and amiable—and how to get into their world and build rapport. I find it difficult to pigeon-hole myself with these models, because I like to think I'm *different*! You may feel the same way, but I think you'll find this model useful for understanding how you deal with other people.

Personality Types

	Passive	Assertive	
Unemotional	Analytical Precise Needs Facts	Driver (warrior) Time Managers	Inflexible
		Magician	
Emotional	Amiable (martyr) Easy going Arbitrator	Extrovert (wanderer) Cheerleader Friendly and Open	Flexible
	Long attention span Make decisions slowly	Short attention span Make decisions quickly	

Figure 9.1

The **Analytical** tends to be unemotional and less active or assertive than either a **Driver** or an **Extrovert**. Analyticals like all of the most precise information they can find before they make decisions. This need for detail encourages a long attention span. An Analytical might subscribe to *Consumer Reports* or at least consult it before purchasing a product. They might also read *Money* Magazine or the *Wall Street Journal*.

The **Amiable** gets along by going along. Amiable people are often martyrs, doing what others want to the exclusion of their own needs. They take a long time to make a decision because they want to make sure that everyone is going to be happy with their decision. They find it easy to arbitrate between two competing factions. They are more emotional and avoid conflict. Amiables like to read *People*.

The **Driver** is a modern-day warrior—unemotional, inflexible, assertive, and driven to succeed. A driver might read this book and try to force the principles to work overnight as opposed to letting them work in their own time. A driver is the ultimate time manager, loaded with DAY-TIMERs and micro-cassette tape recorders and other time-saving devices. They make decisions quickly because they don't have time to waste. They have a short attention span for the same reason, time's a wastin'! Drivers tend to read *Business Week*, *Inc.*, or *Entrepreneur*.

The **Extrovert** leads the cheers for co-workers and lovers alike. They are flexible and emotional, but tend to wander from one exciting thing to another. Like the Driver, extroverts make decisions quickly, using their intuition because they trust life. Extroverts also have short attention spans. They like starting things up, not day-to-day humdrum. They like to read the comics first and magazines like *Playboy* and *Cosmopolitian*.

The **Analytical** and **Driver** are more left-brained. The **Amiable** and **Extrovert** are more right-brained. An Analytical or Driver will need proof of the concepts described in this book. The Extrovert and Amiable will tend to give them a try, but for different reasons: the Extrovert to gain more pleasure, the Amiable to help others get more pleasure.

The softest thing in the universe
Overcomes the hardest thing in the universe.
Those who conquer must yield.
And those who conquer do so because they yield.
—Lao Tzu

Magicians, on the other hand, develop the flexibility to balance all of these styles and use them when appropriate.

In case you're wondering, I'm an Extrovert, not like some that might come to your mind, but an Extrovert all the same. Each personality type can be further subdivided into four quadrants consisting of Analytical, Amiable, Driver, and Extrovert. For example, my personality sub-type is Driver. (Why else would I sit around and pound out a 60,000 word manuscript? Driven!)

Personality types that are diagonally opposite one another have serious trouble communicating with each other. My wife is an Analytical-Amiable. There are times when my Driver-Extrovert personality wants to delegate some of the decision making to her. She'll ask me what I want to do and I'll say, "I don't know. You decide." When this happens, her Analytical side kicks in: "Is something wrong?" Of course, my Extrovert despises analysis (including being pigeon-holed on this chart!). We usually get out of phase when this happens.

Needless to say, I find this evaluation useful when I'm trying to understand where communication breaks down between myself and other people. You may find this useful as well. For example, if you see someone checking their watch frequently, they might be a Driver. Extroverts are obvious; they talk and gesture a lot. Amiables tend to listen. Analyticals almost always look serious. I drive Analyticals crazy because I'm always trying to lighten up meetings with humor.

Knowing only this much about communication styles, you can begin to decide if you want to meet a certain person or not. If you're in a relationship already, this grid can help you diagnose communication problems as they occur.

You'll get along best with someone who is a lot like you. Analyticals like other Analyticals. You'll also get along well with people who border your square on the chart, especially if your secondary personality types are the same. My wife and I, for example, would be better off if I weren't so driven and she were less analytical at times.

Exercise

Compare yourself with your lover, boss, or co-workers. Whom do you get along with best and why?

Now that we know a little about basic personality types, let's take a look at how we communicate with others regardless of their personality.

What Communication?

How do you communicate with others? Do you think you use words? Well, you do, but that's not where the communication happens. We are always communicating. Transfer of information occurs in the following ways:

7%   Words that we can see, hear, feel, taste, or touch

38%   Tonality, rate, pitch and volume of voice

55%   Physiology - body language—eye contact, facial expressions, skin tone, touching, breathing, stance, etc.

We've all heard the expression, "It's not what you say, but how you say it." If you've ever been to a foreign country, for example, you know this is true. Using tonality and body language, you can communicate with almost anyone using the words of your native language. A willing smile and a few simple phrases, like 'please' and 'thank you' will get you almost anywhere.

This is also how we communicate with ourselves. Dale Carnegie said, "Act enthusiastic and you'll be enthusiastic." The mind not only communicates with the body, but changes in the body can communicate with the mind. Studies of top athletes have shown that by adjusting your physiology, tone of voice, and the words you use, you can dramatically change your internal experience and attitude.

Exercise:

Right now, sit or stand up straight. Look up. Breathe the way you would be breathing if you felt unstoppable. Move your arms, hands, and legs the way you would if you felt unstoppable. Say what you would be saying to yourself if you felt unstoppable. Do this for at least 30 seconds and then notice the change in your internal experience.

If you use these tools to improve your internal experience, you will see dramatic changes in your results. If you see someone whom you want to meet and instead of ramping up your physiology you slump forward and hear a tiny voice say: "It will be all right; don't worry," and then you feel a tenseness in your stomach, how are you going to perform? Change your communication with yourself and your results will change with it. Then, if you change your communication with others to more closely approximate the tonality of voice, speed of conversation, and physiology of the person you want to meet, they will bond to you easily. This process is called modeling.

Modeling and Acting

Anyone can do anything; if you model someone who has done it. Modeling is the cornerstone of Neuro-Linguistic Programming (NLP), a method of analyzing the effect of communication, both verbal and non-verbal, on your performance. It originated with Richard Bandler and John Grindner. More recently, it has been brought to wider public attention by Anthony Robbins. NLP suggests that if anyone can do anything, so can you, *if* you can learn to run your mind, nervous system, and body in exactly the same way. If you see a behavior that you would like to have, you can acquire it by modeling it.

Success leaves clues. If you collect the clues and model successful people, you can do anything they do. Personal biographies are a terrific source of clues. If there's someone you'd like to emulate, get all the personal information you can and then model them. A word of caution, however; avoid comparing yourself to others. You aren't in competition with anyone except yourself. Measure your progress and improvement, not your relative position to other people.

Almost every man or woman who achieves romantic success:

1. **knows their desired outcome** (love, sex, marriage);
2. **takes action** to achieve the outcome;
3. and **learns** from what works and what doesn't, and adjusts their approach until they get the result they desire.

Notice what works for you and keep doing it. Notice what doesn't work, and choose not to do it anymore. There is an NLP process called "tape editing" which enables you to do this effectively and efficiently while generating many new choices in your life.

Exercise:

> Take a light-weight experience with a man or woman that didn't work out too well. Notice that it has become a movie that you can rewind at will. Begin from the beginning and play it forward until the first snag appears. Back up before the snag and imagine three new ways you could approach this particular situation. Insert each new choice one at a time and play the resulting movie out in its entirety. Which new choice do you like the best? Store the memory this way. If there are other snags, generate more new choices.

Studying and revising your approach is one sure way to achieve success. Studying others is also essential. To model these winning behaviors, you need to know your:

1. beliefs about relationships;

2. mental strategies for romantic success;

3. physiology—how you breathe, walk, and move your body.

If you build and enhance the beliefs that empower you and take action, you must succeed. If you lean on the weak beliefs and inaction of the past, you will fail. Choose to win! NLP offers another technique to help you develop more flexibility—the New Behavior Generator. It's like trying on a new suit of clothes to see how they fit.

Exercise:

> To begin, pick a role model, someone you would like to be like: a successful friend, Casanova, a vamp from a TV soap opera, your favorite comedian, or a talk show host. At a distance, see this other person interacting with a man or woman in any romantic situation that seems appropriate for you. If you like their results, then see yourself using the role model's techniques and abilities to interact with the same man or woman. If this is still a choice that you would like to have, step into the experience so that you are seeing it with your own eyes, hearing it directly, and feeling what it feels like to use the role model's behaviors. Just by trying on this behavior, it becomes a part of you.

We've already examined how to identify our beliefs based on our results. We've looked at ways to change those beliefs through visualization, thought, and affirmation. We've looked at how people succeed at attracting romance, but we haven't examined their mental strategies and physiology for success. Let's do that now.

Mental Strategies

Each of us has step-by-step ways with which we deal with everything from getting dressed to interacting with people. These are called mental strategies. Did you know that every culture has a courtship procedure of about 30 steps? In America, kissing is step #5; in Britain, it's #25. In 1974, I met a woman at an English wedding and we were kissing before the reception was over. She was a little overwhelmed.

Mental strategies—how we think and act to get results—are based on three key ways of processing information:

1. **Visual** - the pictures we see. These take three main forms: slides, movies in black-and-white or color, or 3-dimensional experiences in sensorama.

2. **Auditory** - words and dialogues we have with ourselves and other people, in varying tones of voice, pitch, and speed. Internal music and background singers can amplify this communication channel.

3. **Kinesthetic** - body feelings that motivate or weaken us.

These strategies are designated in NLP by their first initial (V-A-K). They can occur in either of two key ways: internally or externally (i-e). The sight of a beautiful man or woman, for example, would be designated as *Ve*.

Highly visual people (Drivers and Extroverts) tend to draw pictures, gesture a lot, and talk in high, fast voices. They tend to dress attractively, and drive interesting cars. As they speak, they'll tend to look up and to the left or right as they remember things. They use words like *look*, *see*, and *view*. They say things like: "That *looks* good to me. Do I have to *draw* you a *picture*?"

Auditory people talk in smooth, rhythmic, melodic voices. They tend to look toward their left or right ear as they remember and construct their sentences. They use words like *sound*, *hear*, and *click*. They say things like: "That *sounds* good to me. I *hear* what you're saying. That doesn't *ring* any bells for me."

Kinesthetic people . . . talk in . . . slow, easy . . . phrases. Kinesthetics (Amiables) like soft, comfortable clothes and usually look down toward their right to remember things. They use words like *feel*, *touch*, and *warm*. They say things like: "That *feels* right. I'm *warming* up to the idea." Each of us has a comfort zone surrounding our physical bodies. Kinesthetic people tend to allow people to get closer; visual people keep people farther away.

Any of us can drop into these various states for a while. For example, if you're sick or depressed, you will tend to look down. You know how you talk: "I . . . don't feel . . . so good." A simple cure for this is to sit up straight, breathe deeply, and look up. This short circuits the kinesthetic connection to your depression or illness. I've found that looking up will help stop a cough. Physiology is a powerful tool for personal control.

Exercise

To understand how to develop rapport, you'll need to know your key strategy. Begin to notice what you say and how you talk. Are you predominantly visual, auditory, or kinesthetic?

Besides being an Analytical, Amiable, Driver, or Extrovert, each of us is some mixture of these three types—visual, auditory, and kinesthetic, but one is more dominant than another. I'm predominantly visual.

Exercise

Re-examine the lover, supervisor or co-worker you evaluated earlier. What's their communication style? Does it match yours? What sort of words do they use? How could you change your style to develop rapport when you initiate conversations?

These three styles suggest that people will be attracted to us for a variety of reasons—visual, auditory, or kinesthetic. Look at the advertising and sales strategies on television or anywhere else; they hook us with strong visual, auditory, and kinesthetic hooks. If you understand these simple principles, you'll understand why it's so important to present a strong V-A-K image when you first meet someone. You never get a second chance to make a first impression. We've all seen men and women groomed in visually attractive ways, with melodic voices and a fresh, intimate touch.

Exercise
> Pick someone you admire in this area and model them. Act as if you had all of these things. Put together an image that is consistent with yourself and the men or women you would like to meet.

Visual

Let's imagine for a moment that you're in a restaurant. Across the room you see a man or woman whom you'd like to meet. This person is talking excitedly to his or her friends, gesturing this way and that. What's your guess about this person's strategy? Visual, right? If you wanted to introduce yourself, would you walk up and say in a slow voice, "Hi . . . My name's . . . ah . . . Jay."?

No way. You'd want to get cranked up into a highly visual state, talk fast and gesture with your hands as you speak. By modeling their tonality, rate of speech, and physiology, you can at least get a foot in the door. If you're truly kinesthetic, however, you might question whether or not to approach someone who appears to be so totally different.

Exercise
> List 10 ways you can make yourself more visually attractive to the kind of man or woman you want to meet.

Auditory

Developing auditory power is another essential key to success. Dale Carnegie and Toastmasters can help you with this. Voices can be trained.

Exercise
> Talk to yourself in the mirror using the vocal tone, inflection, and words of first a visual, then an auditory, and finally a kinesthetic person.

When I worked in New Jersey, we had one young woman on our team from Staten Island. She was one of the most delightful, energetic, attractive women you could ever hope to know. Only thing was, she talked like a Brooklyn truck driver. Her accent was as thick as the East River and almost as dirty. A good movie about vocal evolution is *My Fair Lady*; Audrey Hepburn goes from cockney to gentry in 120 minutes. With practice, you can do the same.

What should you do if you can't tell someone's style before you start talking to them? Start in a melodic auditory voice and adjust your style after you hear their speech. Once you've developed rapport, you can drop back into your own style and people will tend to follow you. This is called "pacing and leading."

Physiology

Modeling another person's physiology—breathing, posture, arm position, and facial gestures—is another essential piece of developing rapport.

Exercise
Assume the posture of someone in a bar, coffeeshop, or children's playground. Sit the same way, walk the same way, hold your head the same way, breathe at the same rate, and so on. What thoughts are running through your mind? They'll be similar if not identical to the person you're modeling.

SUCCESS SECRET:
Model the movements and physiology
of successful men and women.

If there's someone you know who's successful at attracting romance, model their movements and physiology. You'll start to think what they're thinking. The physical posture they use empowers them to attract and meet people. Model their courting gestures: eye contact, touching, dancing, walk, and so on. If you can match and mirror their physiology, you've got 55 percent of what you need to succeed.

Empowered people don't walk around in a slouch; they have posture and seem to glide. At rest, they seem totally comfortable, yet poised. They don't walk around with their head bent, scuffing their shoes as they walk. Watch for physiologies that you admire, and model them. I have a friend who has the sexiest, masculine swagger to his walk. When I walk like that, I feel sexy, masculine, and empowered too.

Similarly, we've all seen the swift, stylish walk of a female executive; if you're female and want to be an executive, model her dress and walk. This was well demonstrated in the 1988 movie, *Working Girl*, with Melanie Griffith and Sigourney Weaver. In the movie, Melanie, a secretary, takes over while her boss-from-hell, Sigourney, is laid up with a broken leg. Melanie puts together a $60 million dollar deal disguised as an executive. The only thing she never masters is the vocal inflections of her powerhouse boss.

Next, if you can, model their vocal tonality and speed. Then model their visual appeal. Model as many people as possible to develop flexibility. The more flexible you are, the broader your horizons will become. Trust me; this stuff works.

Success Strategies

Start matching and modeling other people's visual, vocal, and physical strategies, and watch the quality of your communication increase. To further increase your success, you'll need to model people's success strategies. You can begin by doing this with your own life.

Exercise

Remember a time and place where you were completely successful at meeting a man or woman and developing a romance. Take a few minutes. Go back and step into that experience. See it, feel it, hear it. What was the sequence of visual, auditory, and kinesthetic events that triggered your success?

My personal strategy for meeting women *always* followed the same step-by-step process:

1. Ve   I see someone who catches my eye.
2. Ki   I feel attracted to them. The feeling seems to emanate from my solar plexus.

3. Ke   I walk over to them.

4. Ae   I say something funny. Or I say my name
         and then say something funny.

I've examined every relationship that ever worked and I always used this strategy. This probably isn't your strategy. Probably the only person in the world with this strategy, other than myself, is Woody Allen. If I changed the sequence for any reason, for example, if I started thinking about what to say (Ai) before I started walking, I'd break the strategy. Then I'd get caught up in the game of 'What do I say? I don't know! What should I say?' Consequently, I'd miss my opportunity.

If you can figure out your strategy for meeting men or women, you'll never have a hard time making contact, because once you *know* that you know how, you'll start believing in yourself and start doing instead of just thinking about it.

Love Strategies

It shouldn't surprise you that each of us has a strategy for feeling loved. Love strategies consist of one key element—visual, auditory, or kinesthetic—which may or may not be the same as your primary strategy.

My wife feels totally loved when I look at her in certain way. Other people with a visual love strategy may only feel loved if you take them places, buy them things, or show them you love them.

People with an auditory love strategy need to hear certain messages in certain ways. They may need to hear, "I love you," in a whisper, or a soft loving tone, or even a harsh Brooklyn accent. One of my female friends needs to hear a man say, in a somewhat pleading tone of voice, "I need you." As you can imagine, this drives her to some very strange behaviors.

People with a kinesthetic love strategy need to be touched in a certain way. My love strategy is kinesthetic. When I lie on my left side with my head on my wife's right shoulder, I feel totally loved. I've been in relationships where everything else was wrong, but after lovemaking I could curl up, lay my head on someone's shoulder, and feel totally loved. This strategy evolved from when I was a small child sitting on my mother's lap, resting my head on her shoulder.

I'd like to suggest that at times you may have stayed in a poor relationship because that person satisfied your love strategy. If you know what it is, you can get it from any lover that you trust completely, and you can get it any time you want. If you know what it is, you can summon it even when you're alone.

I have another woman friend. Her strategy is to feel supported, as a baby would be, with one hand under the small of her back and one hand under her neck. She loves to dance because invariably, sometime during the evening she'll get to slow dance with at least an arm around her waist and one in the small of her back.

Your love strategy is incredibly powerful. You'll do anything to get it. Without it, you may feel depressed and unloved. Now, let's look at how you discover your love strategy.

1. Remember a *specific* time when you felt totally loved. Take your time to go back and step into that experience. You'll know you've got it when you have the sensation of feeling totally loved.

2. Ask yourself if, to feel totally loved, it is absolutely necessary to:

   a. **See** things, do things, be taken places, given things?

   b. **Hear** certain words or phrases in a certain tone of voice.

   c. Be **touched** in certain specific ways.

3. Remember the specific details of what gives you this feeling. Visuals may respond to roses, or gifts of puppies, or various visual stimuli. Auditories need to hear specific phrases in specific tones of voice—soft, sensual, loud, or whispers. Kinesthetics need to be touched in specific places in specific ways—light, soft, hard, and so on.

When I first did this, I went back to a time when I was nine. I was sitting in my mother's lap and I laid my head on her shoulder. Boom! I felt totally loved. My mother has even said that the day I became too big to fit in her lap was a traumatic day for me. Of course it was. I could no longer get what I needed to feel totally loved. My life has always taken a downward spiral when I couldn't get that feeling in my life. It was a long time from eleven to my first date. So if you have children, find out their love strategy and make sure they get a regular fix.

Love strategies are so powerful. At the beginning of relationships, partners give each other everything—visual, auditory, and kinesthetic messages. That's why we often get the initial burst of love. Later, as we grow comfortable, we slip back into our old habits and start giving what *we want to receive*. If I don't know your strategy and you don't know mine, how can we ensure that our relationship will endure? We can't unless we have the same strategy to begin with.

It's not hard, however, to figure out your partner's strategy and give them what they need, now that you know how. You can even examine the relationships you've had that went bust and understand why they did. Now when your self-esteem dives, you can step back into the experience in the previous exercise or get a friend to give you that powerful message which you need to feel good again.

Whether we continue to feel loved or not depends on certain other internal programs. These are called metaprograms.

Metaprograms

Metaprograms determine how we respond to things in our lives. The most common metaprograms are:

1. how you convince yourself;

2. moving toward pleasure or moving away from pain;

3. internal versus external references;

4. sorting by self or sorting by others;

5. matching and mismatching;

6. possibility versus necessity;

7. independence versus teamwork.

Since we just discussed love strategies, let's look at *convincing* strategies. Some of us will be convinced by a single occurrence of our love strategy. Others will require several repetitions. The rest of us will require continuous repetition of our strategy. I fall into the latter category. Without an occasional fix, I stop feeling loved. With other issues like work related items, I may only need three or four inputs to become convinced. Analytical and Amiable personalities require more convincing than Drivers and Extroverts. What's your strategy for being convinced of things?

Now, let's look briefly at *moving toward pleasure and away from pain* strategies. Wanderers move toward new people, places, and events. Warriors tend to move toward positive things. Martyrs move away from pain through self-sacrifice. Orphans and Innocents move away from pain and instability. Magicians attract pleasureable things to them. Magicians know how to use both pleasure and pain to achieve the maximum momentum toward their desires.

I, for example, tend to move toward things. If one relationship broke up, I'd start moving toward finding another. I love being in love. Other people say, "I don't want to be hurt again." If you say this sort of thing, you probably move away from pain. You may even avoid relationships to avoid possible pain. The only way you can then acquire a relationship is if someone who moves toward pleasure moves toward you. If you move away from things, you'll have a hard time gaining control of your life because you'll find it hard to set goals and move toward them. You'll tend to focus on what you want to avoid, and as we've discussed before, what you focus on *grows* in your life. You may want to change this strategy or change your point of view; instead of focusing on the possible pain of a relationship, you can focus on the pain of being alone—which you'll have to endure if you don't build a meaningful relationship.

Some of us have an *internal versus an external* reference. For example, I rarely rely on the approval of others (external); I approve of myself (internal). Innocents, Orphans, and Martyrs depend on others for approval and love. Wanderers, Warriors and Magicians depend on themselves for approval. It never hurts (moving away from) to get a compliment from someone, but it can be painful to rely on external compliments for self-esteem.

Some of us *sort by* our needs (Analyticals, Drivers and Extroverts) and others *sort by* other people's needs (Amiables). Innocents, Orphans, Warriors, and Wanderers sort by self. Martyrs sort by others, and Magicians have the flexibility of both sorting abilities.

Matchers and mismatchers try to see how things are alike or how they're different. For example, I'm a matcher. I see how things are alike. I'll look at a handful of change and see *round coins from the United States.* Then I see how they are different—pennies, nickels, dimes, quarters, and half-dollars. Mismatchers would say that every coin is different—a penny is not a nickel is not a dime, etc. They might then say that they are alike in shape, but not size.

Have you ever seen those tests that ask you how things are alike? For example what's the next number in the following series:

1 2 3 5 7 11

The answer is 13; they are all prime numbers. Since I see how things are alike, I have no problem with these sorts of tests. They drive my wife crazy. She can't stack two of the same size dishes together or match two towels for the bath. If I didn't know that she was a mismatcher, she could drive *me* crazy because I like order and symmetry. Interestingly enough, clutter (a lack of order and symmetry) makes her crazy, but she doesn't know how to resolve the problem. She tends to throw everything away and start over.

Another metaprogram determines whether you act out of *possibility or necessity* thinking. I wrote this book because of the *possibility* that it would help a lot of people find love and happiness in their lives. You may look for love out of *necessity* or out of a sense of the *possibilities* love could present in your life. This boils down to 'I have to' versus 'I want to.' If you can *move toward* doing things because you want to, your life will blossom more easily. Magicians and Warriors do things because they want to do them. Extroverts do things because they love to do them.

Finally, some of us are more *independent* than *team-oriented.* It's hard to have a relationship without some teamwork. Innocents and Wanderers are independent, maverick-like people. Orphans and Martyrs can't function without others. Warriors always need the assistance of others to succeed. I was a maverick and a Wanderer, and now I'm becoming more of a Magician. I was an only child and grew up believing that I had to do everything on my own. Learning how to build a winning relationship wasn't easy for me, but I found that it could be done. Magicians, again, balance independence and teamwork. I want to become a Wizard at balancing my life.

Exercise:

Determine your metaprograms. Do you:
— move toward pleasure or away from pain?
— think more about your internal experience or
the world around you?
— sort by other's needs or your own?
— notice how things are alike or how they are different
— think more about possibilities or necessities?

We are all products of our environment. These strategies and metaprograms affect how we deal with others and how successful we can be with other people. Use them to examine past and future relationships. They will give you the clues to making your relationships work. They will help you succeed at attracting romance.

Clearing Negativity

Perhaps the biggest blockage to romantic success is the negativity we have built up. Innocents don't have any, but the rest of us do. We all have relationship baggage that slows us down. We've talked about forgiveness as a way to release old relationships. We can also have fear of love and the pain it could bring. Fear is the natural companion of any new experience *if you've never done it before.* NLP offers some ways to begin to clear the negativity you have about success.

Most of these activities are experienced as if you were in a movie theatre. So find yourself in your favorite chair in the middle of your favorite theatre. You are also the projectionist. You decide what to project and how to view it.

Exercise

Take a particularly unpleasant memory that you can't seem to forget and turn it into a movie, a movie in which you have the starring role. Like an actor or actress at the first screening, you will see yourself in the picture rather than what you were seeing at the time. Add a leader onto the movie that included a time just before the experience, a time when you felt safe and calm. Make the movie black-and-white. Now project it on the screen and run it like a movie to the end. Use your favorite music as the background score, eliminating any sounds associated with the experience. Freeze the last frame. Now, step into the movie, change it into color and run it backwards very quickly (2-3 seconds) until you find yourself safe and calm at the beginning. Now step back into your movie seat and run the film clip forward at normal speed. If it has any charge left, step in and run it backwards again at high speed until it becomes simply an experience from which you learned many important lessons. If you did the exercise correctly, you will have cleared the negativity of the experience.

Let's do something else, based on the expression, "He put that experience behind him."

Exercise

Put a still frame of an unpleasant experience up on the screen. Again, see yourself in the picture. Change the picture from color to black-and-white and put an old museum-like frame around it. Now rotate the screen around the theatre until it's behind you. See the screen move off to the horizon behind you. See the picture get dim and blurry and finally disappear.

From an NLP standpoint, this will push your problems further away from you and actually "put them behind you!" You can use the reverse process to relive your past successes—bring one up big and bright and full of color right in front of you, seeing it from your own eyes.

This can also be accomplished with a technique called a *swish* (Figure 9.2).

Exercise

See the movie screen filled with a picture of some unpleasant experience or behavior with a person from your past. Practice having this picture shrink down to a tiny dot. Similarly, think of an image of the you who has all of the abilities and skills required to be fabulously successful in relationships. If you can't think of one, make one up. In the bottom right-hand corner, left-hand corner, or center of the picture screen, see a small dim picture of this positive person you'd like to be instead. Practice having this screen get larger, brighter, and more vivid and colorful until it fills the screen. Now put the smaller image on top of the larger unpleasant image. In one or two seconds, as the larger image shrinks, bring the smaller image up so that it bursts through the negative one. Make it big and bright and full of color. See yourself enjoying the love and companionship of someone special. Feel what you'd be feeling and hear what you'd be hearing. Repeat this seven or more times.

The Swish

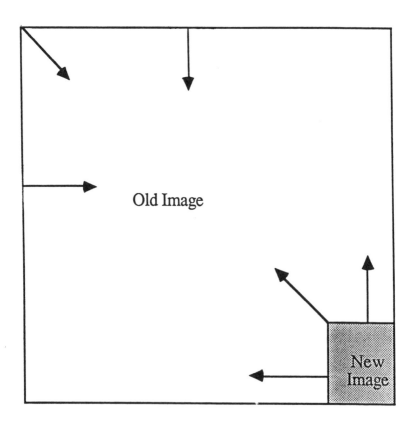

Figure 9.2

These exercises will help reframe your old experiences and create the desire for new ones. The human brain always selects the most positive state, the most powerful program. Nothing has any meaning except the meaning and power we give it. With these few tools you can change your perspective of any situation. No matter how bad a situation, you can always represent it to yourself in a way that empowers you.

Everything is programming us for either success or failure. If you haven't been succeeding, it's because of your programming. As you learn to run your brain, body, and nervous system in powerful ways, you'll begin to succeed magnificently at attracting and developing romantic relationships.

Chapter Ten

Come to the Cabaret

> **SUCCESS SECRET:**
> Nothing happens if you're a hermit.

SUCCESSFUL PEOPLE DO THINGS THAT UNSUCCESSFUL people are unwilling to do. You can practice with the magician's tools in this book, but unless you get out in public, you'll have a hard time finding love, romance, and happiness. Conversely, if you get out of the house but fail to visualize, affirm, and think about your success, you'll still have difficulty finding your perfect mate. If your warrior goes out and tries to corral men or women, you'll most likely overlook the person who's right for you. They're usually smart enough to avoid the Viking approach to mating.

> **SUCCESS SECRET:**
> Eliminate the concept of
> aloneness from your life.

You are never alone unless you choose to be. You can change your own mind. Successful people do several other things to ensure their success:

149

1. Study how to succeed.
2. Maintain their intent to succeed—
   desire, belief, and acceptance.
3. Create situations where they can succeed.
4. Sell themselves.
5. Take action to succeed.
6. Persist.
7. Have patience while waiting for the Universe to arrange
   their future.

To succeed, you will need to continuously work in all of these areas. If you accomplish just one thing you thought was absolutely impossible, it will reinforce your self-esteem and cause you to rethink your beliefs.

Study and Learning

Why are you reading this book? To learn skills that will help you develop the romance you so richly deserve. Do I have all the answers? No! There are wonderful biographies of successful men and women. There are books on relationships and love. Read! Study! What can you learn from others?

We're all brought up to believe that there is one right answer:

1. Your prince arrives on a silver stallion and
   whisks you away.
2. Your princess kisses you and the ugly frog
   turns into a prince.
3. Love at first sight!

Ah, if it were only so easy! First we have to learn. We learn how to succeed by watching and studying and mimicking others. The experienced lover, like a great tennis player, has achieved grace—the ability to respond to every situation naturally and gracefully. This ability comes from hours of practice, trial and error, trial and success. Watch people who are having fun meeting other people; mimic them, model them. They are in the mood to have fun! Why bother studying people who look glum or disinterested?

Failure

Twenty percent of whatever you do will generate 80% of your results. The other 80% of what you do will produce either feedback or marginal results. Learn to be a pessimistic optimist. The more things that go wrong, the closer you are to the 20% that will bring you all of the romantic rewards you can handle.

I'd like you to imagine a funnel (Figure 10.1). If you begin today to meet one new person a day, it will act like a funnel. As you pour in new contacts at the top, relationships will begin to flow out of the spout. If nothing is coming out, it's because you haven't been meeting enough new people. If bad relationships are coming out, it's because your old thoughts and beliefs attracted some men or women that weren't right for you. It may take some time to clear these out of your funnel and get strictly good relationships flowing out into your life now.

Because of the vast number of people we all know, we're only seven people-links from anyone in the world. Someone you know often knows someone who would be a perfect match for you. As you meet people, male or female, ask for referrals! Like golf, you may zig zag around the course and it may take you many tries, but eventually your golf ball (desire) must find the cup (your romantic goal).

Keep track in your notebook of the people you meet. If it takes meeting seven people to get a date, you can think of everyone you approach as one-seventh of a date. This is one way to handle the fear of rejection. See every *outcome* as bringing you one-seventh of a date. If you knew that every seven contacts would bring you one date, I know you'd be out there meeting seven new people a day. If out of every five dates with different men or women you get one serious relationship, you'd be motivated to meet so many people that you could go out every night of the week. Remember the funnel. Meet everyone you can find. Someone wonderful must appear!

And now a word about rejection. Earlier I said that the Universe always asks you to pay the cheapest price for anything you want first. Rejection is a cheap price if you compare it to the cost of developing a poor relationship with someone that you'll never enjoy. Be thankful for rejection! Look at what it saves you!

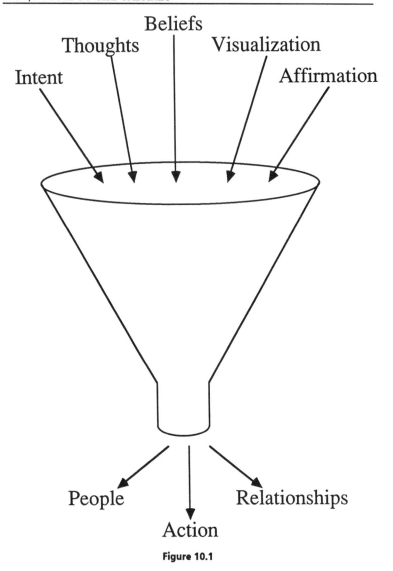

Intent   Thoughts   Beliefs   Visualization   Affirmation

People   Action   Relationships

Figure 10.1

Maintain a compassionate attitude toward yourself and your learning process. To the extent you can do this, the learning process
becomes fun and interesting (even though it may seem painful at first).
When I was first learning how to ski, I was so bruised and embarrassed
from hitting the snow that I never wanted try again; but, I reasoned,
millions of people can't be wrong . . . there must be some fun in this

somewhere. Soon it became possible to ski the beginner slopes and enjoy the view. Now I enjoy skiing. I can manage expert runs if I have to, but I stick to intermediate ones. I recently went through the same trauma learning to play golf. In each of these instances, I learned from a professional instructor, trial and error, and trial and success.

In forming relationships, however, I always felt ill at ease because there were no instructors. It's like handing someone a pair of skis, taking them to the top of the mountain, and saying, "See you at the bottom." This book is an owner's manual which helps you exercise your native abilities to succeed at romance.

Now as I look back at my relationship history, I can see what I did right and wrong. But I never examined it until recently. To admit that you don't have natural abilities doesn't mean that you can't learn to play reasonably well. This is the first step toward success. Once you assume a beginner's mind about developing good relationships, you begin to loosen the grip of your beliefs and begin to learn. When you let go, you become what you might be; you receive what you need most.

The Zen master, Shunryu Suzuki said: "The mind of the beginner is empty, free of the habits of the expert, open to all communication. When we have no thought of achievement, no thought of ourselves, we are true beginners. Then we can really learn something. In the beginner's mind there are many possibilities, but in the expert's mind there are few." (Suzuki, 1970) If you open up to the possibility that finding love, romance, sex, or marriage is easy, you will find simple ways to ensure that they find you. This book has many simple exercises to encourage your growth.

For the beginner, however, practice without effort is not true practice. For the beginner, practice often takes great effort. If you've ever tried to learn a new sport after the age of thirty, you can see this clearly. Part of the difficulty comes from the part-that-drags. We actively resist new, unknown thoughts, ideas, and activities because we do not know what we do not know! We secretly know that we are unconscious incompetents.

Once you try a sport, however, you quickly discover how incompetent you are. You become a conscious incompetent—you know that you do not know, but you commit yourself to study, practice, and learning. As your skill develops, you become a conscious competent—you can produce good results, but you still have to think about them. Finally, after a period of time, the learning sinks below conscious awareness and you become an unconscious competent. For example, have you ever driven from home to work but had no recollection of how you got there? Unconscious competence.

Becoming successful at attracting romance will follow the same path. The beginner's mind can see things as they are. Step by step and sometimes in a blinding flash of the obvious, you can realize the original nature of everything. If your mind is empty, it is always ready for anything. It's open to everything. This zen-like state brings you into awareness of yourself. You simply apply what you already know and find that love becomes effortless and spontaneous. Don't even think about meeting someone; just do it. Tennis players never think about hitting a ball; they just do it. As you practice the art of the magician, you will learn to meet people without effort because you will peel back the layers of beliefs that block your natural abilities, revealing the innocent part of you that knows how to meet people easily. We've all seen a baby who can look us right in the eye, lovingly, as if we're the most interesting people in the world. When we can regain our ability to do that, we will meet people easily, anywhere we go.

Intent

We know that if we don't plan our life, someone else will plan it for us. We have to choose a design for our life. It has been said that the pain of discipline weighs ounces, but the pain of regret weighs tons. First we must figure out what we want (goals), then plan and act to reach those goals. As we move toward what we want, we must maintain our intent—desire, belief, and acceptance.

To succeed, you must take action. The first steps should be little ones that create little successes. The journey of a thousand miles begins with a single step (in the right direction). Find low risk, positive things that you can do to attract romance. Do them often. You can talk to your waiter or waitress, people on street corners, in elevators, wherever. Do enough low risk things that succeed and you'll soon be able to do higher risk activities. The sooner you start getting some of what you really want, the more energy you'll have to go for the rest of it.

Respect your own pace. Don't push yourself. Trying too hard only produces unwanted results. Remember, you should feel a little discomfort as you grow, but you shouldn't have to exert a tremendous amount of effort to succeed. Expect some resistance as you go; the part-that-drags will try to slow you down.

Establish a clear intent to attract a great relationship into your life (even if it's just for one night). Recognize all of the assets you have that will help you attract this romance and give thanks that you have them.

Remember to use your intuition. If you see someone and they keep popping up in your life, go meet them. Many years ago, there was a woman who was so startlingly attractive that my mind just went blank when I saw her. (I couldn't follow my strategy.) We were obviously interested in each other, but I couldn't think of a single thing to say and she never approached me, either. We saw each other in many places all over town, but never did meet. I've always wondered what we missed. In every other case where I was attracted to someone and kept running into them, I always attempted to at least meet them. Most of these encounters turned into at least a date or two. Trust the Universe; it's always encouraging us. Repetition is one of its ploys.

The Land of the Lounge Lizards

> **SUCCESS SECRET:**
> Find the fast flow.

We can help the Universe by deciding where we want to spend our time. Looking for love is like looking for gold—if you look in the same old places you'll find the same old tapped-out veins. Be curious. Poke around in new areas. You may hit the mother lode.

Most of us have "one right answer" about where to meet romantic partners—bars, health clubs, work, church, wherever. If you believe you can only meet your perfect mate in one place, you'll never notice the opportunities that await you in your local supermarket, or on a street corner, or in the business section of your local library, or even at Taco Bell!

Use your internal barometer of comfort and discomfort to decide when you should initiate contact. If it feels comfortable, do it. If it doesn't feel good, don't do it.

Do what you love, and love, romance, and sex will follow.

Exercise
In your notebook, brainstorm 50 possible places and ways to meet new men or women. List 50 places and 50 ways that you normally wouldn't consider. Don't edit these ideas. Just jot them down. Have fun!

Here are a few ideas:
Sunset in the park
Biking
Picnic
Art museum
Free Concerts
Coffee and rolls in a diner
Old fashioned Ice Cream parlor
Hiking

Once you have a huge list of places, you can begin to evaluate them. Some ideas will be better than others. Never throw out an idea until you ask yourself:

1. What can I salvage from this idea?
   Would it be a fun place for a date?

2. How can I get around the impractical elements?

3. What further ideas does this suggest?

Every idea can be a stepping stone to a better idea. Remember the story of the man who met sensual, sexual women in the lobby of a free VD clinic? Step out of the usual to encourage the magic in your life.

Rhythmic exercise is another way to dredge up ideas. Jog or walk to relieve stress and open up your creativity centers. While the body is occupied, the mind can roam at will.

Using the beginner's mind, you can stay constantly aware of opportunities to attract romance. So what if it's not where you normally meet men or women? A friend of mine met a fabulous woman in the parts department of a Honda motorcycle dealership. You're far more likely to meet someone with similar interests doing what you love to do than if you stick to the same old haunts.

Once you figure out where to look for the love of your life, you'll need to learn some sales skills to help ensure your success.

Salesmanship

SUCCESS SECRET:
Nothing happens until someone sells something.

You have to sell yourself. Whether you're attracting a mate, a friend, a business partner, or anyone else, you will have to sell yourself. You must become your own salesperson. This means that you must excel in the quantity, quality, and spirit of love, sex, or compassion that you provide. Sell something you love; sell yourself!

I'll bet that you bristled at that last paragraph! Everyone seems to hate salespeople. That's because we believe that salespeople are often taught to manipulate the buyer into buying something they really don't want. Do you believe that selling yourself is ridiculous? Well, if you believe in what you're selling, you owe it to everyone to sell it. You're performing an invaluable service! How else will people know that you exist?

Remember, you don't need to manipulate others; you create win-win situations for your partners and yourself. You are learning to help someone else get what they want. If you can help enough other people get what they want, you will get what you want. If you're in a bad relationship, you can help the other person get what they want by setting them free, getting out. Staying in a poor relationship helps no one. You can only succeed in romance through the cooperation of other human beings.

SUCCESS SECRET:
People aren't looking for you; they're looking for the feeling they'll get from being with you.

Some people want to be seen in beautiful cars with beautiful women or handsome men. Some want to feel the warmth of a lover's arms around them on a hayride. Everyone has different needs. If you don't believe me, take off your shoes and walk a few miles in a woman's high heels or a man's Florsheims.

SUCCESS SECRET:
People buy for emotional reasons and then justify it with logical ones.

When it comes to sex, some people want the feeling of closeness with another person; some people want the feeling of orgasmic release. When it comes to love, some people want the burning thrill of love and others want companionship.

As you start to meet people, if you follow your intuition, you'll find that you usually meet people who can win from building a relationship with you. It may not last forever, because it will take some refinement to get your perfect person and perfect life defined and in place, but you can learn from each other and grow.

Exercise
Mentally thank all of your previous lovers for what they taught you about yourself and about life.

How to Get Whatever You Want

Most people are afraid of asking for things, and when they finally do, they don't insist enough. That's a mistake.
—Mark Fischer

Ask! The Bible says: "Ask and you shall recieve." Talk to someone. Ask them out. Ask successful friends what they do to attract and build relationships. They are usually happy to tell you.

Of course, you need to learn how to ask intelligently. This means asking:

1. **specifically** - using the perfect person exercise;

2. **someone who can help you** - someone who looks, sounds and feels like your perfect person or someone you would like to model;

3. **someone you can help** in return;

4. **with belief** that you deserve romantic success;

5. **until** you find someone who can help you.

Be prepared if success comes suddenly. Expect the unexpected.

When you first try this, you may feel as if you're stepping into the abyss. The best and most exciting way to learn to meet men or women is by doing whatever comes to mind. I once got a dozen roses from an admirer at work. "The Lady in Red," she signed the card, but the flowers were delivered a couple of days late because I wasn't at home to receive them. No one ever asked, "Did you get my flowers?" I've always wondered who she was. I'm sure she wore a red dress the day after the flowers were supposed to be delivered, but I didn't notice because I didn't know.

```
SUCCESS SECRET:
Be Bold!
```

Doing this takes nerve, but the rewards are phenomenal. You know how far you can go only by going too far. If you are ready to listen, your intuition will give you lots of wild ways to make contact. Listen! It is the readiness of mind that is wisdom.

There are several types of risk takers:

1. people who take no risks;

2. people who take poorly calculated risks;

3. people who take well-planned risks and succeed.

If you try to approach someone who's been sending you "get lost" looks, you're taking a poorly calculated risk. If, however, you start conversations with lots of people and see how the communication goes before you think about asking them out or getting into bed with them, you'll be able to take well-planned risks and succeed. If you're comfortable talking with someone, it bodes well for the relationship. If not, you're in trouble.

For example, I used to eat breakfast at the company cafeteria. One morning I paid for my breakfast and carried my tray out into the middle of the room and there, sitting alone, was a remarkably attractive brunette. Without thinking, I walked over and said, "Hi, can I join you? I hate eating alone." Sure, she said. We tried a number of topics that failed and finally turned to movies. She said, "I hate Woody Allen. He reminds me too much of the Marx Brothers and I *despise* the Marx Brothers."

There must have been an audible gasp. Woody Allen and Groucho Marx are the cornerstones of my humor. I said something ridiculous like, "I think I hear my mother calling," and I got up and left. There was nothing more to say.

Another time, a friend and I had been sailing all day and stopped outside of the Black Pearl bar in Newport, Rhode Island, to have a beer. There were two women sitting on the sidewalk. I looked down and said, "You know, you short people have no reason to live!" It was a popular song at the time. To my surprise, they stood up and we had a great evening together.

SUCCESS SECRET:
You must take chances to achieve great success.

Trust your instincts. Try wild and crazy things, or simple, ordinary things—whatever works best for you.

Remember; what you can do, do it; what you dream you can do, begin it. Boldness has genius, power, and magic in it. Take action. Use the famous time management phrase: "Do it now!" Take constant action in the direction of your goals and you cannot help but succeed. Whatever you've been putting off—why wait for the timing to be right? There's no time like the present, so do it now. If you think you need to learn how to dance to attract a new mate, do it now! You may meet them at the studio. If you think you need a new haircut, a new car, a new religion, or a Master's degree in Clinical Psychology, do it now!

Successful people take action. This is the key to personal power. Aristotle said that courage is the first of human qualities because it is the quality that guarantees the others. In the *Wizard of OZ*, the Cowardly Lion overcomes his fears to be courageous, the Scarecrow discovers his brain, the Tin Man shows his compassion. Whatever trait you fear you do not have, you probably have in abundance; you simply haven't tapped it yet.

To tap your hidden resources, set a deadline for making your first contact. Until you're committed, you'll hesitate, draw back and act ineffectively. You'll make excuses and dredge up all of your strategic patterns for avoiding success. Above all, don't think. Meet people from a state of potent emptiness: no thought, no mind, no form, just emptiness. A thought is 1000 times slower than action. The most potent response is not conscious, but spontaneous. Respond to what is happening here and now without calculation or manipulation.

To succeed at attracting romance, each of us will use several archetypes: the explorer, the artist, the warrior, and the judge. To succeed, we use these roles *in order*. Using them out of sequence or using one too strongly will short circuit our success.

The explorer seeks the "best places" to mingle; the artist dreams up the best approach; the warrior takes action to bring the person into their lives; and the judge evaluates the person.

If you start to analyze someone before you've met them, it's easy to get stuck in the judge's role: "He's too tall; too short; too smug or too glib." This is just a way to avoid taking a risk; all you have to do is disqualify someone before you meet them: no risk. Call this paralysis by analysis. Similarly, your artist can build a person into a god or a goddess that your humble, human warrior would never dare to meet.

Or your explorer can drift from place to place or person to person, never settling long enough for your artist and warrior to take over.

If you see someone and feel that you want to meet them, go do it. Then let your judge analyze the results of your interaction *after* you've had some time to talk.

SUCCESS PRINCIPLE
The secret of success is constancy of purpose.
- Benjamin Disraeli

Or, as Newton put it, a body in motion tends to remain in motion. A body at rest tends to remain at rest. If you haven't been meeting people, it's going to take some energy and effort to get going. Once you begin, however, it takes only a little effort to continue in motion. Develop a rhythm of meeting people. Keep your funnel full.

Make effective use of your time. The way you spend your time is the way you spend your life. You can't meet people curled up in front of the television. Make the best use of every occasion and situation you encounter. If you're in the dentist's waiting room, make it pay! Be aware of everyone around you. It doesn't matter where you are; meet someone. Learn their name and repeat it to them. Dale Carnegie says that a person's name is, to them, the sweetest sound in any language.

Exercise
Meet five new people and learn five new names a week for five weeks.

SUCCESS SECRET:
Give yourself time to succeed.

Most people are lazy, greedy, and self-centered. This is neither bad nor good; it just is. We'd all like instant gratification, but that's not the way the Universe works.

Refuse to be frustrated. Frustration wastes energy. So does worry, either about being alone (for the rest of your life) or about meeting someone. Take a breath. Relax. Be patient, or use frustration and worry as the catapult to encourage you to take action. Unpleasant emotions can be a powerful force for action.

It's Always Too Soon To Give Up

People usually fail when they are on the verge of success.
So give as much care to the end as to the beginning;
Then there will be no failure.

—Lao Tzu

As you start working on finding and building relationships in your life, all hell may break loose. The negative relationships you have waiting in your funnel may suddenly fall out as you start putting good contacts into the top. Things may get worse before they get better.

SUCCESS SECRET:
It's always too soon to give up.

Persist! Keep going. Be like the ocean that comes back again and again, wearing away the shoreline which cannot move to resist it. As you persist, you'll accumulate the skills and the people necessary to satisfy your dreams. It's like being in a fog; you don't know you're getting wet, but as you keep walking, you get wet little by little. Respond creatively to the problems that present themselves, and believe in yourself.

Recognize that everything you do succeeds in producing a result. If it doesn't work, try something else (Figure 10.2). If one person says, "No thank you," to your advances, try another. You never get used to rejection, but every rejection brings you closer to success.

Exercise
Once a week, go for rejection. Try to meet someone who you thought was totally out of your league, and be prepared for success.

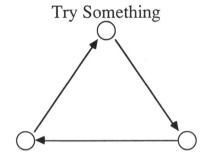

Try Something

Improve Approach   Analyze Results

Figure 10.2

I always found that attractive women were far easier to meet because they were more comfortable about being approached. Their beauty often scared men away. If you're attracted to someone, give it a shot. You might just succeed, and wouldn't that be heaven?

I was skiing in Sugarbush, New Hampshire. It was late in the day and my friend wanted to go up for one more run. I decided to pack it in. I kicked off my skis and went into the lodge. I bought a beer and looked around for a place to sit; there were none! Then I spotted a fabulously attractive brunette sitting all alone. I walked over and asked if I could sit down. She gave me a distracted "sure." As I sat down, I noticed her designer scarf; it had ruby red lip prints on it with signatures like Monique, Michele, and so on. I asked her if she always autographed her kisses. She laughed. It turned out that she was a stockbroker in Boston, skiing with her current boyfriend. She gave me her card and told me to call her if I ever got up to Boston. Magic! (Notice that I followed my V-A-K strategy.)

If you fail, it's no big deal. Profit from your losses. Mistakes don't mean you're bad. Reframe what they mean to you. Look for possible benefits from each meeting. Nothing has any meaning except what we give it. No matter how bad things go, you can always represent it to yourself in a way that empowers you. Failed encounters help you learn. View each "failure" as an outcome. Decide what kind of outcome you want:

1. State your desired outcomes in positive, specific terms:
   "I have a date for Saturday night."

2. Decide what constitutes evidence of having achieved this outcome. How will you look and feel when you've achieved your goal?

3. Verify that you truly want this outcome. Remember, the gods may give it to you!

As you begin to succeed, try not to be greedy. When your effort is greedy (trying to get what you want), you will become discouraged with it (because no one will help you). You've got to help others get what they need—the *feeling* they get when they're in love.

He Who Hesitates Waits

He who hesitates is a damned fool.
— Mae West

Timing *is* everything. I can't count the number of times that I've been attracted to someone and had my judge start critiquing the person (not following my V-A-K strategy). By the time I'd told my judge to shut up, some other man had beaten me to the woman I wanted to meet. I unnecessarily beat myself up about this. The Universe wouldn't have allowed it to happen if it wasn't in my best interest, but it still bothers me. If your effort is in the right direction, there is nothing to lose. Give it a shot.

It's amazing how you will find solutions and support when you commit to romantic or any other kind of success. When I was unpublished, a friend of mine suggested that I send a publisher a chapter and a table of contents. "What's the worst thing that could happen?" she asked. "They might say no," she concluded, "but they might say yes." So I tried, and I was published. The same is true of developing relationships.

As you practice meeting people, you will develop a wonderful power. Before you attain the ability to meet people easily, it will seem wonderful; but after you acquire it, it will seem like nothing at all (unconscious competence).

> ## SUCCESS SECRET:
> Let go in order to succeed.

You may also find, after trying hard to find love, that when you finally give up and stop working at it, you will find love and achieve spectacular heights of success. Security can only come from trusting that everything will work out perfectly.

The truth often sounds paradoxical.

> *Yield and overcome; bend and be straight;*
> *Empty and be full; wear out and be new;*
> *Have little and gain; have much and be confused.*
> *Be really whole, and all things will come to you.*
> —Lao Tzu

Letting go to achieve success may sound paradoxical, but by letting go you stop thinking and start acting instinctively. When you approach someone, you will burn yourself completely; you won't be a smoky fire. In order to master attracting romance, we need to release all attachment to it. Let go of your efforts to be successful; such efforts only block your success.

Live in the moment. Do or do not, there is no try. If you spend too much time warming up, you'll miss your opportunities. Do you know anyone who has to get skunk drunk in a bar to approach someone?

Then again, if you don't warm up at all, you may not finish. Instead of diving in cold, take a minute to do what any good salesman or Olympic athlete would do:

1. Take a deep breath, hold it to the count of four, and release it slowly. This will relax you.

2. Affirm silently: "I'm the best! I'm the best, warmest, most loving person anyone can ever hope to meet! This man/woman joyfully accepts my advances. I'm the best!"

3. Preplay your meeting. See yourself relaxed, at peace, calm and confident. Imagine yourself getting larger and your ener-

gy radiating around you and around the person you're about to meet.

4. Imagine the end result—the man or woman smiling and talking and enjoying your company. See them giving you a phone number or joining you for coffee or dinner. Feel how you will feel when you succeed!

These steps will put you in the frame of mind that encourages success. Now take action:

1. To initiate contact, start with whatever comes to mind. Follow your intuition. I've said things that range from: "You short people have no reason to live!" to "Hi, my name's Jay." Men and women all love a fresh, honest approach.

2. Small talk can increase tension! Talk from the caring heart and loving child in all of us, not from the mind. Follow your intuition!

3. Listen! Don't interrupt or phrase your next casual remark. Just listen! People like to talk about themselves.

4. Avoid arguments. Show respect for the other person's thoughts and ideas.

5. Smile and use the other person's name.

If you preplay your success and then follow your natural instincts, you can't go wrong. You don't have to be someone you're not. Just be who you are and success is yours. You won't succeed with everyone, but you will succeed with people who will be good for you.

Exercise

The Blitz. Anyone can do anything for 30 days. So for 30 days do everything you fear to do to initiate contact. If you're female, ask men to dance, ask them out, pick men up. If you're male, talk to everyone, ask for love, ask for dates. Have fun. Try everything that you're afraid to do. Be outrageous! You just might be surprised.

At the same time, do several exercises from the book every day. Repetition is the key to imprinting these techniques in your mind.

SUCCESS SECRET:
Double or triple your failure rate.

The best cure when you're discouraged is to double or triple your efforts. Keep looking for another way or another approach to success. Don't waste too much time on methods that don't produce results. Keep on trying new approaches until you run out of things that won't work. Somewhere, at the end of all of those approaches, is something that will bring you the *Wizard of Oz* experience. Magic happens.

Rewards

SUCCESS SECRET:
The fastest way to change your behavior is to stop rewarding negative habits and start rewarding positive ones.

Women, how many of you go on shopping or eating sprees when a relationship doesn't work out? You're rewarding exactly what you don't want to happen. Realize that there is no right or wrong to relationships. You've learned and you're better for the experience. Reward yourself for building solid, new relationships.

Men, how often do you reward yourself with drink after drink in a bar for *not* approaching the woman of your choice?

Stop rewarding the wrong kinds of behavior, the wrong kinds of habits. Start rewarding yourself for working toward success. Start rewarding yourself for success!

Exercise
Choose some rewards, both tangible and intangible, that would be important to you for achieving even the tiniest goal:
Buy yourself Haagen Dazs ice cream for getting someone's name.

Pay yourself five dollars for every phone number, ten for every date, and so on. When you get enough money, give yourself something luxurious—a full body massage, a night in a luxury suite at a hotel, whatever. Design some one-minute self-praisings for small steps. (Pat yourself on the shoulder and congratulate yourself for talking to that man or woman in the elevator.)

By creating a reward structure, you will begin to reinforce everything you do right. The child in you loves toys and rewards. As you learn to reward it for good behavior instead of bad, it will go out of its way to bring magic into your romantic life.

Go for it! Loving magic awaits your first step, your first action.

Chapter Eleven

In the Groove

*The key to success isn't much good until
one discovers the right lock to insert it in.*
—Tehyi Hsieh

I LIKE TO COMPARE RELATIONSHIPS TO AIR TRAVEL. It
starts with the slow taxi of initial communication and small talk. At
the edge of the runway, the couple are cleared for takeoff. One or
the other starts the relationship rolling; it gathers momentum; at any
sign of danger, either one can shut it down and both are watching all
of their internal gauges. Gently, ever so gently, one person pulls back
on the yoke and the relationship lifts off the ground and accelerates
toward the sky. This is the initial rush of falling in love . . . the feeling
of love's gravity slamming you back in your seat as the magic explodes
within you. It takes a lot of energy to get a relationship up to 39,000
feet, but it always seems as though you have the energy reserves to
meet the need.

At some point, however, you level out going 600 miles per hour,
and it seems as though you're hardly moving. (A body in motion tends
to remain in motion.) With subtle corrections, you can keep the
relationship on course and growing. You can also decide to go ballistic
and accelerate past the speed of sound, rising higher and higher.
Again you get the burn of high-intensity love. Can your love leave the

grip of earth's gravity and weave its spell on the Universe? I don't know, but I'm going to find out.

On the other hand, at the first plateau, the man or the woman may forget to feed the relationship enough energy to keep it at altitude, airspeed and on course. Both the pilot and the copilot can forget to watch the instruments. Or the fire of love can burn out. When this happens, there's normally some spin-crash-and-burn relationship disaster. Most of the people I've met who avoid establishing relationships focus on the fear, pain, and hurt of a lost love. The obvious alternative is to set the partnership down gracefully, shake hands and move on, or find some way to keep your relationship growing and climbing through the stratosphere.

Or you may run into one of the four types of Casanovas, either male or female:

1. thrill seekers who thrive in the fast lane of love, using love as a drug;

2. game players who live for the game (e.g., the movie *Dangerous Liasons*) and keep track of the "score";

3. escape artists who, like Houdini, get imprisoned and then escape;

4. devouring men and women who consume their conquests (e.g., the movie *9 1/2 Weeks*).

A Casanova can make you feel as if he—or she—just lit the candle under the space shuttle and you're the astronaut. These men and women see people as consisting of two types: those to run from and those to pursue. At the center of their love and sex addictions is the vacuum of low self-esteem.

The real Casanova, Jacques Casanova de Seingalt, slept with 122 women in 39 years. His latter day counterparts are driven by love-hunger and frustration. They are repeatedly seductive, unfaithful, abandoning, and addicted to sex. Few men or women can resist their elusive challenge. They often brag about their other conquests as if to say, "Catch me if you can!"

If you meet one of these rare individuals, run, do not walk to the nearest exit!

Sometime in your life, however, you have to stop running, take a relationship opportunity, and go all the way to commitment. Don't be so worried about losing in a relationship that you never take the risk; take the chance, the rewards are incredible! Once you find such a relationship, you will want to continue to use all of the tools in this book—visualization, affirmation, and positive thought—to make it grow and to diagnose what's working and what isn't.

Exercise:

Stand up and imagine your time line on the floor in front of you. Step onto the time line facing your future and walk back five years into the past. Begin to notice and write down what you could have done to improve the quality of the relationships you've had. Write down what you could have done to make them worse. Step back up into the present.

Exercise:

Write down what you have to lose from not having a relationship and then write down what you have to gain from building one. Notice your current behavior with men or women. Now step back onto your time line.

1. Imagine for a moment that you continue to develop the same old kinds of relationships and step five years into the future. How do you look? How do you feel? How have you changed? Step back to the present.

2. Now imagine that you've become a magician capable of attracting healthy relationships into your life now. Again, step out five years into the future. How do you look now? How do you feel? How have you changed? Go out ten or twenty years. How do you feel now? What can you do to make this an even deeper, richer experience? When you're ready, step back into the present.

For those of you who did this exercise, you probably noticed major differences in the quality of your life. For most of us, we saw a happier, healthier, more balanced person in the future.

Relationships are the best self-help course in town. If you're willing to learn, your partner will be your guru and you can be theirs. Even your parents, siblings, and co-workers can be teachers, if you let them.

The magician's power can increase when used by two or more people. Use this power in your relationship to manifest beauty, love, money, and riches of all kinds in your relationship. Use this energy to empower your evolution.

The Past

Taking things lightly results in great difficulty.
Because the sage always confronts difficulties,
He never experiences them.
—Lao Tzu

Relationships continuously evolve. As they evolve, you should recognize that you're probably toting around some emotional baggage that filters your experience of your current relationship. Your *perception* of and *reaction* to your relationship, either positive or negative, can do more to harm it than any other thing. If your perception is too positive, too bright, or too cheerful, you may overlook things that need correction, like a pilot who ignores an engine warning light. If your perception is too dark or negative, you'll tend to over control even the tiniest fluctuations in your relationship. No matter how big or small the problem, there's always a way that you can both correct course and win in the relationship, even if that means landing your ship gracefully and moving on to other people. Stay aware. Retain the beginner's mind.

SUCCESS SECRET:
Your emotional past is an illusion.

Your romantic past no longer exists, but it can cause you to be cautious or to take chances that you need not take. It can cause you to be demanding, to expect more than your mate can deliver. The past does not have to color your future. See your lover clearly instead of through the veil of the past. Every loving thought is true. Every loving thought is real; everything else is illusion. Fearful, angry, or hateful thoughts are illusions. Angry thoughts are only a means to make others (or yourself) feel guilty.

Why live in the past when you can live in the present and experience the joy of a warm, loving relationship. Use forgiveness to eliminate your connections to the past. Forgive every lover of the past who has "hurt" you. Forgive your current lover as well. Use the techniques in this book to release the negativity of past encounters and to enhance the wonder of positive ones. Keep the magic of your relationship in front of you at all times; put the negatives behind you.

Exercise:

Take any unpleasant experience from the past and change it by following these steps:

1. Step out of the picture so that you can see yourself in the experience.

2. Change the picture into black and white, put a frame around it, and move it back away from you so that it gets smaller and dimmer.

    Now take a pleasant romantic experience and change it by following these steps:

3. Bring the picture closer, make it bigger, brighter, panoramic and vividly colorful. You can even fill it with sparkling light.

4. When the picture seems irresistable, step into the experience and enjoy it. Notice what you are seeing, hear what you are hearing, feel what you are feeling. Fill out the experience in any way that makes it richer for you.

If you do this with enough positive and negative experiences, your brain will learn how to code these experiences and it will do it for *all* of your memories. Use the good part of your past, the part that makes you feel proud and strong and full of self-esteem. Take the negative charge off the part that didn't work. You learned from those experiences and you know better now, don't you?

In the Beginning

We all experience the rush of a new relationship, when everything seems new and exciting. Do not confuse excitement and arousal with the flow of love. Excitement is just passing desire. Vital energy springs from love. If we remain open, this continues and accelerates. Recognize that events are manageable and can be corrected easily in their beginning phases; every problem begins small and simple, and every desirable trait can be encouraged. Don't wait until heroic action is needed to set things right. Improve your relationship every day.

As we put ourselves emotionally at risk, however, we can begin to cling to the relationship. We may try to hold on to what we've got, and that's when the magic starts to slip away. We start to lose those initial feelings of love and wonder.

The initial experience of falling in love is so powerful that we often spend years trying to recreate it. Some of us become addicted to it and go from relationship to relationship for those six months of glory. The harder we try (exerting effort instead of going with the flow), the more it eludes us.

What do we do then? We try to hold on even harder, squeezing the life out of the relationship. A friend of mine used to say, "He who binds himself to a joy, doth the wings of life destroy."

When this happens, let go. Trust the Universe to provide. It will. What you try to hold on to will slip away. Let go and it will return if it's right for you. Only when you give up and let go can the energy start to flow through you again, putting you in touch with the love that flows through everything.

Develop a zen-like quality of recognizing the energy in everything you do, even simple work. The beginner's mind does the dishes, walks the dog, and starts the laundry. By doing these things and finding pleasure in the process, you will grow in your relationship every day. Retain your beginner's mind and your relationship will stay fresh and young.

The Present

SUCCESS SECRET:
Success is a journey.

Once fully formed, let your relationship grow and expand. Don't get eager for specific outcomes—marriage, sex, or commitment; allow them to unfold naturally. In a sense, we are all wanderers. Developing successful relationships is a journey, an adventure, not a destination. When you meet someone, you haven't arrived, you've just begun. When you get married, you don't have to freeze up like an old pump in winter; you can change and evolve to stay in alignment with the Universe and your lover.

The key to success is to acknowledge your needs, ask for what you want, and give your partner whatever he or she desires in return. Changes in relationships can be painless and beautiful when we communicate honestly and trust ourselves. Our mates are willing to give us what we desire and we are willing to give in return. The continuous giving and receiving opens up the channel to love. If you're truly honest about your needs, things will work out so that everyone gets what they want. Getting what you need doesn't mean that someone else has to do without.

Remember, what we give multiplies and comes back to us. Give your mate lots of psychic income, recognition for doing the simple things—chopping wood, carrying water, doing dishes, walking the dog. Reward everything you want to see grow with words of loving praise. Watch your lover perk up like a daisy in a spring shower.

Learn to share the power in a relationship. Wherever one force dominates, another force will resist. This is the nature of the universe. The *Tao Te Ching* describes this in exquisite detail. Learn to balance the power in your relationship and watch your love blossom.

Another technique for giving your partner what they want is to mirror their actions. What they do spontaneously for you is exactly what they want you to do for them. I, for example, give out hundreds of back and shoulder rubs a year; they happen to be my favorite non-sexual touching behavior. I love to receive back rubs in return. Similarly, if your lover repeatedly looks at you in a certain way, talks in a certain way, or touches you in a certain way, *that's how they want to be treated in return.*

The man who approaches his partner by touching her sexually probably wants to be touched in the same way (even if his approach turned the woman off because it was too direct). She, on the other hand, may plan a romantic candlelight dinner with wine as mental and visual foreplay. (Listen up guys. She's trying to tell you something.) Mirroring your mate, date, partner, or spouse is an effective way to ensure that you give them what they want from your relationship.

On another level, use the magician's tools to change your relationship. Use visualization, thought, and affirmation to get what you need. See your spouse as more loving, or touching, or sexual, or whatever you need. If you'd like to go dancing more often, set goals, create a plan, take action, get some lessons, get a baby sitter, get out there and have fun. Grow, grow, grow.

Conversely, if you imagine the man or woman in your life having affairs with other people, you will start acting in ways that will force them to have affairs with other people. People turn out the way you expect them to turn out. The reason people get divorced is because they focus on their few incompatibilities instead of giving thanks for all the things they have in common. (I hope I've given you the tools to assess a relationship's potential long before you decide to get married. If you aren't sure, use your intuition. If you can't see, hear, or feel what it would be like to be married to this person, you're not ready.)

Getting Out

```
SUCCESS SECRET:
Let go of what isn't working.
```

Not all relationships are destined to last forever. Don't major in minor relationships. If a relationship isn't working, if you're putting out a lot of *effort* to make it work, do yourself and your partner a favor . . . get out! Get out now.

I once dated a woman who was brilliant. She knew where she was going in business and where she wanted to go in her personal life. She was intent on going right to the top of the management chain, getting married, and having children at the same time.

We'd go out, have dinner, party with friends, and then we'd go back to *her place* and I'd spend the night. In the morning, it was as if I were a foreign element. She used to say that she had to start putting on her corporate armor, because otherwise the men would chew her up. It was a little bit like going to bed with Dorothy and waking up with the Tin Man. I knew I couldn't live like that, so I got out. She's now a vice president with a loving husband and children. We both learned from that relationship and I know that we both won.

Remember that most relationships end the way they begin. If your relationship went up like a ballistic missile, it may auger back into *terra firma* the same way. If a relationship starts badly, it may end badly as well. Fortunately most of my relationships have started well and ended gracefully. Remember that when you go with the flow, relationships will begin and continue almost effortlessly. When you're swimming against the flow, however, you may need to reevaluate what you're doing and decide to move on to a more rewarding love relationship.

Most people hate to abandon a bad investment, whether it's a car or a love relationship. After all, look at how much we've invested in this rusty heap! You must learn how to cut your losses. Free yourself quickly of a relationship that does you no good. All true lovers want to win. Don't waste your time and your life in a losing relationship.

Side Dishes

The man or woman in your life may be the main course, but you can't have a very satisfying meal based on one basic food group. You'll need side dishes and desserts.

Build friendships with men and women in other areas. See your independent interests as fodder for continued growth of your relationship. Your mate only has a certain amount of experience that can be brought to the relationship. Through others, you can enhance what each of you brings to the relationship. You're here to help each other grow and expand. When you stop growing you're in a rut, and a rut is just a grave with the ends kicked out.

If you see your relationship as a center for learning and growing, you'll always desire to continue. If you take it for granted and stop growing, you've sown the seeds of its failure. Care for your relationship as you would any crop. Take care to plant the seeds of growth, water them and weed out negativity. If you do, your love will nourish your emotional body as the fields nourish your physical body.

You deserve to be strong and healthy and loved!

Chapter Twelve

Life Balance

I WAS AN ONLY CHILD. I excelled in school and got good grades. I spent the first half of my life "pumping mind." Somewhere in my head is a bunch of grey matter that looks a lot like Arnold Schwartzenegger. I gave little thought to balancing the physical and spiritual sides of my life. A kidney stone and other exciting changes made me reassess what I was doing. Now I've begun to explore improving my physical health and my spiritual awareness. I'd like to share with you some of what this has done for my life and ways to use the magician's tools to achieve success in other areas of your life—financial, career, personal, professional, and private.

It is important to seek a balance in every aspect of your life. Successful people know the critical importance of a balanced life. They look for a symmetry of body, mind, and spirit. They work toward equilibrium in their personal (family), private (self), and professional (career) growth. They search their relationships for a growing balance of love, sex, and companionship (Figure 12.1).

If you want to succeed in all areas of your life, you need to think of success as a process, a journey, a way of life, a habit, and a strategy for the rest of your life. It's not just a one-time shot. Success is something that you must apply in all areas of your life if you expect to succeed at romance.

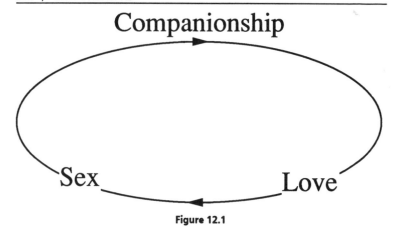

Figure 12.1

SUCCESS SECRET:
The only real success is to be able to
spend your life the way you want to spend it.

Let's face it—your fairy godmother isn't coming, or she would've put in an appearance by now. Doing what *you* want isn't selfish; it's the key to living a successful life.

Somerset Maugham said, "It's a funny thing about life; if you refuse to accept anything but the best, you very often get it." Expect the best from yourself, your friends and your lovers, and you usually get it.

The world is meant to be a playground. Yet people seem to be divided between soarers and plodders, those who look at the sky and those who stare at the ground in front of them. Be a soarer, like Jonathan Livingston Seagull.

SUCCESS SECRET:
Goals work in all aspects of your life.

The keys to success are: always know what you want, take action, and persist until you get what you want. Quitters never win, and winners never quit.

At first as you strive for success, it will seem as though you change very little and accomplish even less. Yet, if you shift your direction in life by only one degree, you will—in just a few short weeks—be infinitely closer to your goal than if you'd stayed on the same old heading, the same old course. As you learn to change your direction even more, you'll find yourself curving quickly to the goal you desire. Reward yourself for success, but never be satisfied. Keep on improving yourself and your life.

In most of this book, we've discussed attracting successful relationships, a personal goal. I believe that emotional success is essential to personal success, but you need to balance other areas of your life as well.

Personal-Professional-Private

If romantic success is one of the keys to personal success, you will also need to develop personal and professional friendships and work relationships that help you grow and that give you new things to keep your romance growing (Figure 12.2).

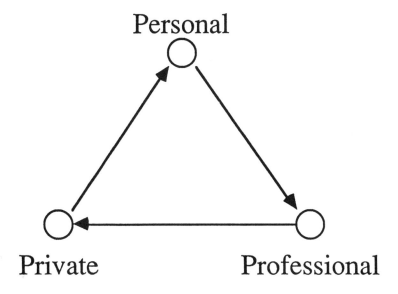

Figure 12.2

In your professional life, you'll need to develop working relationships with mentors, supervisors, and peers that encourage your success. The tools in this book work for developing friendships and mentors alike. They can help you attract a dynamic new job or find people to support you when you start a new business. They can even attract customers to your business!

Exercise

Take 30 minutes and, in your notebook, write your professional (career) and financial goals. State specifically how much money you want in the bank, how much you want to earn, how much you desire in *passive* income from investments or other sources, and what kind of job or activity you desire to do in return for these rewards.

Write a plan to move toward these goals. Include lots of simple steps you can do today. Do one now!

All you need to do is develop the intent—desire, belief, and acceptance—for a new job, friend, boss, or mentor, and follow the stairway to success—purpose, goals, plan, action, persistence. If it is in your highest interests, what you want will appear, like magic. I've used these tools in this way and all kinds of interesting things have occurred in my life. In one case, a woman called to ask if she could pay me $1,000 to reprint an article I'd published two years before. Originally I was paid only $300. In another case, a man called to say that he enjoyed my first book about computers so much that he wanted to put me in touch with a friend who heads a cable network. All I did was to figure out my personal, private, and professional goals and do the following exercise. If you'll do it every day for 21 days, it can easily repay the price of this book.

Exercise

First thing every morning for 21 days, write your personal, professional, and private goals. Take a moment after writing each goal to richly and vividly imagine what your future will be like when you've achieved the goal—see it, hear it, feel it! Bring it closer, make it brighter, add exciting music and background singers.

I earn $40,000 a year. See your paycheck. Hear your supervisor say, "Good job!" Feel your pride at a job well done.

I supervise 8 people. See your employees working well. Hear their appreciation for your leadership. Feel your pride at helping them succeed.

You'll be shocked at the results, in just 21 days. If you want to be rich, I recommend beginning with the book, *The Richest Man in Babylon*. The formula is simple:

> **SUCCESS SECRET:**
> Ten percent of your income is yours to keep.

Save ten percent of your income and invest it in diversified, safe investments. If you can't save ten percent, start with one percent. Every time you get a raise, save a little and reward yourself with the rest. Increase the amount you save. In 1973, I started in the company savings plan; I saved six percent of my income. Twelve years later I had almost $100,000.

> **SUCCESS SECRET:**
> Make money work for you!

Use your savings to buy investments that generate money you don't have to work for; make your money work for you. You may be tempted to spend this money, but don't do it. Use your work income to finance your day-to-day needs. If you do this, you'll be able to live off the income stream 10-20 years down the road.

> **SUCCESS SECRET:**
> Save as if you're going to live forever.
> Spend as if you're going to die tomorrow.

I had two friends who started doing this in college. Fifteen years later, one man and his wife retired to Maui. Last Christmas I got a card from Nepal. My other friend, Gale, was on a two year trip around the world. *The Richest Man in Babylon* gave them the key.

Add little to little and you have a big pile. Learn to save and invest a little of what you earn and in a few years you'll be able to take an extended trip around the world or just kick back and enjoy life. Do it! Ten percent (or more) of everything you earn is yours to keep.

Money is like love; the amount you have usually equals the amount you're willing to receive. Don't be afraid to circulate the rest of your income. Imagine the money you spend as enriching the whole Universe, multiplying and returning to you ten times over. Don't be a scrooge about giving to charity. If you try to hang on to all of your money, you're focusing on lack and you'll attract more of it. If, on the other hand, you have enough money to give some away, you'll give your mind and the Universe a clear message that money is abundant in your life. You'll attract more.

Body-Mind-Spirit

In your private life you'll want to establish a balance of body, mind, and spirit (Figure 12.3). Medical science has proven the importance of positive mental health, thought, and visualization on the survival rate of cancer and Aids patients. I can tell you that what you think can change the frequency of illness in your life.

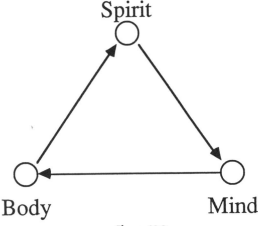

Figure 12.3

In 1985 I was fatigued and stressed out. I had a running cold that refused to leave. I left the company and spent a year writing, but the colds and flu didn't leave. I grew a kidney stone and scared the heck out of myself. I caught myself saying the affirmation: "I'm sick and tired of being sick and tired." That's when I *decided* that I didn't want to be sick anymore. I developed the *intent* to be healthy.

Once you have the intent, doors will open for you. I was browsing in the Tattered Cover bookstore in Denver when a number of books about healing seemed to jump out at me. I discovered a self-hypnosis tape on self-healing that helped as well; the relaxation exercise helped me sleep while the medical community was trying to diagnose this simple kidney stone and I was scared silly from the blood in my urine. These books and tapes taught me the importance of *preventing* illness. Now, every morning, I get up and repeat the following:

I feel good! I feel great! Every atom, every cell, every muscle, every nerve and every fiber of my being is now made whole, pure, and perfect by the healing intelligence in my subconscious mind. I give thanks for the healing I know is taking place now.

Exercise

Affirm this every day for 21 days and find out if your health improves!

Often, when we can't seem to deal with life, we catch a cold so that we can rest. It's much easier, I've found, to get up every day and fill your mind with healthy thoughts. I started by studying healthy people, people who have recovered from illnesses, like Louise Hay. I started saying, "I am willing to change," and entered into a variety of positive programs for improved health. I haven't caught a cold since.

Trouble is easily overcome before it starts.
Deal with it before it happens.
Set things in order before there is confusion.
—Lao Tzu

Disease (dis-ease) is our bodies' message that we are not following our true energy and feelings. At first, we get easy clues, like colds. Remember the Universe always asks us to pay the smallest price first. If we don't heed those clues, it gives us something more expensive, like a kidney stone. If we let it go on long enough, we can develop heart disease or possibly cancer, but it's never too late to be healed if we have the *intent* and follow the stairway to success.

Robert Dilts, one of the co-founders of NLP, helped his mother recover from what doctors described as a "terminal" case of cancer. He says it is no accident that we call the abatement of the dis-ease *re-mission*. To get a new lease on life we all need a reason for living—a new *mission*.

You can lose weight the same way. Pick a target five pounds below your current weight and affirm, "I easily release five pounds and I now weight xxx pounds. I look wonderful." As you write this affirmation, let your negative responses surface: "No you don't. You love to eat too much to ever weigh xxx pounds." As they come out, they will lose their power over you. Then visualize yourself at the lower weight. As soon as this mental program overtakes the dominant program that controls your weight, you'll lose those pounds for good.

Similarly, if you'd like to exercise, but hate the thought of it, use the affirmation I discovered to reprogram my mind to enjoy exercise:

Exercise nourishes me. Exercise heals me.

Say this as you walk, run, jog, or kick up your heels in aerobics. Imagine your slim, muscular body six months, one year, and five years in the future. Soon you'll be in love with exercise, just as when you were a kid who ran all day and rode a bike the rest of the time.

Exercise, health, and physical fitness are a few of the keys to personal power and, therefore, success. What you eat can also affect your energy and power. You may notice that after you eat certain kinds of foods, you get a charge of energy that lasts and lasts. If you inhale a cola, however, you may get a quick rush and a quick let-down. Other foods may cause an immediate decline in power and energy.

Wake up! Your body is trying to tell you something. Listen. Wait till you're hungry and then eat what you feel like eating. Watch the response you get. You'll soon discover what foods tune you up and which put you down. To attract romance, you need to be at your best. Food is another key to personal success.

Male-Female

We all have both male and female, yin and yang aspects to our personality. Know the strength and warriorship of a man, but retain a woman's caring, intuition and wizardry. A man or woman who achieves balance of male-female, body-mind-spirit, and personal-private-professional is a true magician.

Exercise

Using Figure 12.4, write down everything you're doing for your body, mind, and spirit via your professional, private, and personal life. When you're done, which boxes are empty? Create five new ways to integrate these areas of your life.

Personal Balance

	Body	Mind	Spirit
Professional			
Private			
Personal			

Figure 12.4

This balance of all things is often refered to as enlightenment. Enlightenment is a clear vision of the perfection in all things and everyone. There are many ways to seek balance and enlightenment; two of these are meditation and prayer.

Meditation

SUCCESS SECRET:
Calmness of mind is the jewel of self-discovery.

Learn to meditate. Top athletes have discovered that to be at their peak, they have to have time to rest and regenerate. Steven Jobs, co-founder of Apple Computers, meditates frequently. The purpose of meditation is to quiet the mind and to learn to pay attention at even the most unextraordinary times. By taking some quiet time you'll often be able to solve the puzzles of your life and work miracles to correct them.

Doctors are using meditation to combat serious illness; you can use it to insure that you stay healthy. It will also help you attain your goals in life much more quickly. Meditation helps clear out the fears, worries, and clutter of daily life. It gives you a chance to stand on top of the mountain and see your life clearly.

Exercise

Take 20-30 minutes, put on some instrumental music, take a few deep breaths, count backward from ten to one, and let your mind grow quiet for a few minutes. Then bring a problem or challenge into your mind and examine it. See what revelations come to you. They will.

Prayer

Where meditation is a journey within yourself, prayer is a direct request to God and the Universe. When you can't find an answer to your relationship needs by looking within, ask a divine force to reveal what you need to do next. Prayer is simple and can best be accomplished by repetition of four key steps:

1. Invocation - "God/Universe, hear me!"

2. Give thanks - "I give thanks for the many fulfilling relationships in my life!"

3. Problem/focus - "Please help me understand (whatever the problem might be)."

4. Affirm - "I now believe and accept the fulfillment of this request."

As always, release any concern about your problem or question. Be patient and the answer will come to you easily and effortlessly when the time is right. Remember to repeat your prayer every day in the same way until an answer appears.

Balance

As you start to achieve a balance in all areas your life, you will discover a balance in your emotional life as well. Lovers are made, not born. As you learn to open your heart, you will always have enough love. Giving love away tells your mind that you have love in abundance and it will attract more to you. As you give up old patterns of behavior by doing the exercises in this book, you will find your vital life and love energy released.

You may find that the part-that-drags doesn't want to do these exercises. It's saying, "There must be an easier way," or, "I don't want to change." I challenge you to give this book and its exercises a chance to work miracles in your life. To know yourself takes wisdom. To manage your own life takes true power! Your future is of your own creation. Create wisely!

Love always heals the person who dedicates his or her efforts to its directions. Love who you are, where you are, what you are doing, with whomever you're doing it. Give thanks for the abundance in your life, and let magic fill your life forever.

Appendix A

The Affirmations of Love

Relationships

I am the creator of my life.

I am responsible for my life.

I radiate my goals every day, I visualize them every night,
and then my dreams reinforce
the achievement of my goals.

I am willing to change.

All of my negative thoughts and beliefs dissolve effortlessly.

I always attract satisfying relationships.

I now attract the perfect lover for me now.

I love and accept my perfect body, mind and spirit.

I am beautiful/handsome and sexy.

I expand my comfort zones easily and effortlessly.

I fully and freely forgive everything
and everyone who has ever hurt me.

I enjoy my body. I enjoy my sexuality.

Love is eternally present.

Everyone always approves of me.

Everyone always accepts me.

Relationships always work out exquistely.

The more I take intelligent risks, the more I succeed.

I fully and freely accept perfect relationships in my life now.

I am a totally loving and lovable person.

It's safe to allow people into my life now.

I am willing to trust my intuition.

I am an artist and my life is my greatest work of art.

My intent is focused to create perfect relationships now.

I desire, believe that I deserve, and accept love in my life now.

People love my company.

I am loving and wonderful.

I treat everyone I meet as
the most important person in the world.

When I change and succeed,
the world changes and succeeds.

Every relationship I have pays off handsomely,
either in satisfaction, or valuable experience.

I radiate success, love and enthusiasm.

No matter what I do, my relationships multiply.
Finding and building my perfect relationship
    supports rightness in the whole world.
Perfect people flow into my life now.
Everyone loves me when I attract great relationships.
Every negative thought I have
    automatically triggers three positive ones.
I am self-assured whenever I meet someone new.
I surrender to the natural rhythm of the Universe.

Health

I feel good! I feel great!
I feel the power of the Universe flowing through me now.
I heal myself.
I am energized, alive, and filled with radiant health.
I can live as long as I want. Every cell in my body *youths*.

Financial Affirmations

I deserve to have everything I desire.
A lot more money flows to me now,
    for the good of all concerned.
I love what I do.
I am an unlimited reservoir of valuable ideas.
Every dollar I spend enriches the universe
    and returns to me multiplied.
My financial worth increases everyday.
I am rich and wonderful.
People love to give me love and money.

Appendix B

Quick Reference

Deep Relaxation

1. Take a long, slow, deep breath, hold it for the count of five, and, as you exhale, count slowly from ten to one.

2. Do this three to five times.

Creative Visualization

The steps of creative visualization are:

1. Get a clear picture of your goal.

2. Imagine the end result. Feel it!

3. Clarify your desire. How much do you want this, specifically?

4. See yourself in the picture. Add action, emotion, sight, sound, smell, taste, and touch.

5. Repeat these four steps often. Strength can be developed only through repetition and effort (Figure 5.1). The more you rehearse your experiences, the greater your chance of success.

6. Lock out conflicting images.

7. Give thanks *as if* what you want has already appeared.

New Behavior Generator

1. Pick a role model, someone you would like to be like: a successful friend, Casanova, a vamp from a TV soap opera, your favorite comedian, or a talk show host.

2. At a distance, see this other person interacting with a man or woman in any situation that seems appropriate for you.

3. If you like their results, then see yourself using the role model's techniques and abilities to interact with and develop romance with the other person.

4. If this is still a choice that you would like to have, step into the experience so that you are seeing it with your own eyes, hearing it directly, and feeling what it feels like to use the role model's behaviors.

Tape Editing

1. Identify an experience that didn't work out too well.

2. Make it into a movie that you can rewind and replay at will.

3. Begin from the beginning and play it forward until the first snag appears.

4. Back up before the snag, look up and to your right, and imagine three new ways you could approach this particular situation.

5. Insert each new choice one at a time and play the resulting movie out in its entirety.

6. Notice which one feels the best, which one would be appropriate in future situations.

Appendix C

Resources

Creativity
von Oeck, Roger, *A Kick in the Seat of the Pants*,
New York, NY, Harper & Row, 1986.

Dreams
Bethards, Betty, *The Dream Book*, Novato, CA,
The Inner Light Foundation, 1983.

Garfield, Patricia, *Creative Dreaming*, Los Angeles, CA,
Audio Renaissance Tapes, Inc., 1988.

Health
Hay, Louise, *You Can Heal Your Own Life*,
Hay-House, 1984.

Journals
Goldberg, Natalie, *Writing Down the Bones*, Boston, MA,
Shambahala, 1986.

NLP
Bandler, Richard, *Frogs into Princes*, Moab, UT,
Real People Press, 1979.

Robbins, Tony, *Unlimited Power*, New York, NY,
Fawcett, 1986, paper. Audio Cassette available
from Nightingale-Conant, Chicago, IL.

Bandler, Richard, *Using Your Brain for a Change*,
Moab, UT, Real People Press, 1985.

Dilts, Robert, *Walt Disney*, Santa Cruz, CA,
Dynamic Learning Publications, 1990.

NLP Comprehensive, 2897 Valmont Road,
Boulder, CO 80301, 303-442-1102

Metaphysics

Gawain, Shakti, *Living in the Light*,
San Rafael, CA, Whatever Publishing, 1986.

Mythology

Campbell, Joseph, *The Power of Myth*, New York, NY,
Doubleday, 1988.

Pearson, Carol, *The Hero Within*, New York, NY,
Harper & Row, 1986.

Relationships

Ray, Sondra, *Loving Relationships*, Berkeley, CA,
Celestial Arts, 1980.

Success

Tracy, Brian, *The Psychology of Success*, Chicago, IL,
Nightingale-Conant.

Sinetar, Marsha, *Do What You Love and the Money Will
Follow*, New York, NY, Paulist Press, 1987.

Patent, Arnold M., *You Can Have It All*, Piermont, NY,
Celebration, 1987.

Sher, Barbara, *Wishcraft*, New York, NY, Ballantine, 1979.

Tao

Tsu, Lao, *Lao Te Ching*, various.

Heider, John, *The Tao of Leadership*, New York, NY,
Bantam, 1986.

Thought

Allen, James, *As A Man Thinketh*, New York, NY,
Grosset & Dunlap.

Visualization

Gawain, Shakti, *Creative Visualization*, New York, NY,
Bantam, 1978.

Zen

Suzuki, Shunryu, *Zen Mind, Beginner's Mind*, New York, NY,
Weatherhill, 1970.

Personal Biography

Lowell Jay Arthur

Lowell Jay Arthur is a husband, father, teacher, and author living in Denver, Colorado. As a Certified Master Practitioner of Neuro-Linguistic Programming (NLP), Jay specializes in personal and organizational growth and evolution. Through improved communication and personal transformation, you can achieve both your personal and professional destiny. Courses are available from :

LOWELL JAY ARTHUR
c/o Distinctive Publishing Corp.
PO Box 17868
Plantation FL 33318-7868
(305) 975-2413

Additional copies of
ATTRACTING ROMANCE
by Lowell Jay Arthur
may be ordered by
calling toll free 1-800-683-3722
or by sending a check or money order
for $17.95 postpaid for each copy to:

Distinctive Publishing Corp.
PO Box 17868
Plantation FL 33318-7868

Quantity discounts are also available
from the publisher.